Dominoes
and Other Stories

Other  titles

Speak
Laurie Halse Anderson

Festival
The Last Virgin
Denial
David Belbin

Blood Money
Anne Cassidy

Last Chance
Dreamland
This Lullaby
Sarah Dessen

Magenta Orange
Magenta in the Pink
Diamond Geezers
Blaggers
Echo Freer

Guitar Girl
French Kiss
Kiss and Make Up
Sealed With a Kiss
Pretty Things
Sarra Manning

Blue
Reckless
Voices
Poisoned
Sue Mayfield

Superhuman
XY
Boy Kills Man
Matt Whyman

Dominoes

and Other Stories

Bali Rai

*Hodder
Children's
Books*

A division of Hodder Headline Limited

First published in Great Britain in 2005
by Hodder Children's Books

A Catalogue record for this book is available from
the British Library

ISBN 0 340 87732 4

Typeset in TimesNewRoman by Avon DataSet Ltd,
Bidford-on-Avon, Warwickshire

Printed and bound in Great Britain by
Bookmarque Ltd., Croydon, Surrey

The paper and board used in this paperback are natural recyclable
products made from wood grown in sustainable forests.
The manufacturing processes conform to the environmental
regulations of the country of origin.

Contents

Dominoes

'It's a party, Mum. One of the girls from school is having it.'

I waited for a reply.

'Girl? School?'

'Yeah, Mum. School.'

My mum thought for a moment and then asked me if I wanted any more food.

'Nah, I'm full, Mum. Can I go?'

'What time it finish, beteh?'

'Dunno – eleven. Twelve. Round then.'

My sister walked into the living room and picked up the remote. She sat down and flicked channels.

'Well . . . ?'

'OK – but you be back by twelve. Your sister will be alone otherwise.'

My sister snorted.

'We ain't kids no more, Mum. I'll be fine. And

he'll be fine. Just go to work.'

My mum worked nights at a local supermarket, filling the shelves ready for the morning. She had worked the same job for years. When I was a kid she'd finish around two in the morning but the supermarket got bigger and opened for longer now so she had to work through the night. Not that she was bothered. More hours meant more money which meant the rent got paid and the gas and electric meters stayed whirring. And then there was the phone bills and the food and everything else. And even then it only just about covered everything. The trials of the single parent, man. Wack.

My mum gave me a weary look.

'OK – you go but any messing about and that's end of you – *gettit*?'

'Yeah, yeah,' I replied, dismissive as only a fifteen-year-old can be.

My sister snorted again.

'*Bet* you won't get into trouble,' she said, eyeing me suspiciously.

My mum sighed and got up from the settee, pulling on her coat and grabbing her workbag which contained a couple of chapattis, some lentil dhal in a silver container and a flask of tea. Same meal every night for years.

Unless it was someone's birthday or Diwali or Christmas or something. Then she'd make pakora and samosas and maybe even a bit of tandoori chicken. Chicken was expensive though, so not that often.

'Can I borrow some money please, Mum,' I asked, not really expecting anything.

'I got two pound in my purse – and to *borrow* money beteh – you have to give it back.'

'I'll get a job on Saturdays – I promise,' I said, taking the money out of her purse.

'Right – be good and I see you tomorrow,' she said, making her way to the front door, dismissing my promise. I heard the door open and then slam shut. My sister stood up.

'Right you little shit head – where are you really going?' she said, raising an eyebrow.

'Get lost,' I replied, ducking as she swung for me and missed. I laughed and pulled a face at her.

By the time I was ready, all neat hair and *criss* clothes and that, my sister was watching EastEnders and on the phone to one of her friends. I never got how she watched TV and talked to her mates at the same time but she told me it was a girl thing – being able to do two things at

3

once. She's older than me, my sis, by a couple of years and she works part time and goes to college – to finish the GCSEs she messed up at school. Back then she was too interested in boys and clothes. As I walked into the room she eyed me up and down.

'You ain't going to no school 'ting dressed like that – where you headed?'

'Mind yuh business,' I replied, checking my hair in the mirror over the fireplace and then plonking myself down on the settee with force.

'See – you never learn, do yer? Tell *me* or *I'll* tell Mum.'

'Ah come on sis – I never tell Mum when you go out all night . . .'

My sister smiled.

'That's 'cause, officially, I don't,' she replied.

'Well, I still don't mention it.'

'You're forgettin' the small matter of that weed that I found you smoking. And the night that you had that Misha in your bedroom . . .'

That was the way things were between me and my sister. Everything was an exchange. Do this because I did that. Don't say this because I never said about that. Like them primitive barter economies that history teachers like telling everyone about. You know – '*they used to swap one of their goats for someone else's socks.'* Yeah right – fascinating man.

See, because our mum worked nights, and our dad had died when we were so young, we got to have a little bit of freedom. But it was all based on favours. One night my sister might be out till late with her mates or some boy or other and I'd cover for her. Not say anything to Mum. In return that gave *me* one night – *in lieu*, they call it – that I could have without worrying that my sister would snitch on me. And once we had started this little agreement, it was like we were building dominoes. Setting them up like we were trying to get the world record. All our nights out stood in line. That was why we'd never tell on each other. If either of us said anything then the other would tell too, and boom. All the dominoes would come crashing down, one by one. Better to just leave things the way they were. And we both knew it.

Which made our little game before I went out pointless. Pointless but fun. It was tradition.

My sister relented.

'Go on – get lost – you know I ain't gonna say anything anyways,' she said, smiling.

I went over and gave her a little hug.

'I know,' I told her, 'later.'

I grabbed my stuff, keys and wallet and that, and made for the door.

The house my mum owns is in the middle of an inner city. There's crack dealers down the end of the road and prostitutes working twenty-four seven. The kids round here walk the streets all night, in their little gangs, facing each other off and fighting and stuff. In a way they play the same game as me and my sister – dominoes – only out on the streets it's more dangerous. One lad calls some other lad's sister a nasty 'ho' or brags about how she gives good head and that – and before you know it the brother has gone home, picked up a knife and gone and cut up the bwoi making the accusations. But it don't stop there . . .

The one who gets attacked wants revenge so him and his mates do over one of the other crew – most likely the bwoi who did the stabbing or his best mate – and then you have two dominoes. Next, there's another bit of revenge and before you know it the dominoes are standing in line like tourists waiting to go see the Crown Jewels. And some time them dominoes are bound to fall . . .

Anyway, I made down the street, heading for the bus stop where one of my best mates, Jamie, was supposed to be. Jamie was never on time though so I knew that I'd be the one doing the waiting. The night was cool but not as cold as October can be, when you get that nasty chill and you can't stop shivering and your teeth start to chatter. I got to the bus stop in two minutes and I sat on one of the plastic seats, lit up a fag and waited. And waited.

Ten minutes and two buses after I got there a crew of four lads cruised by in a stolen car. I knew it was stolen because one of the lads hanging out the passenger window – Yusuf – went to my school, and I knew he was into taking a ride in a next man's car. I ignored them as best I could but they were staring right at me. Seeing if I would make a move. One of them made a show of flipping open his phone and calling someone. Another one of their crew. Probably.

The one making the call was Mo – another kid from school, only he had got suspended and then excluded. I shivered slightly, thinking about the time Mo and Jamie had got into a fight outside the local fried chicken place. Set up their own domino when Mo pulled a blade and Jamie used another to cut Mo right across his ugly face. Mo was even uglier now. And full of the need for retribution. It was an ongoing feud. One that had started when we were all Year Sevens. And it had just grown worse over the years – to a point where it was deadly. And that change from playground fights to full on street shit was all down to a single pair of trainers. But that's a different story.

The car pulled away down the road and round the corner as yet another bus sped by the stop. I pulled out my own phone and called Jamie.

'Yeah – where the fuck *are* you, man?'

'*On my way, bro. Hold your horses.*'

'Mo and them just took a swing by the bus stop . . .'

'*What? They try anything, Dal . . . ?*'

'Not yet, J, but they will.'

Something clicked on the line.

'*Step over to the cab stand across the road – I've got Reese with me – be there in two, man.*'

The call ended.

I got up and walked quickly across the road, dodging between the traffic. Someone shouted out at me, a scooter papp-papped its horn, and then I heard the screeching of tyres. I looked down the road behind me and saw Mo and his mates coming up the road, driving straight at me. I ran for the pavement, jumped to reach it. They only just missed me by an inch or two. I stumbled across the uneven paving and fell into the cab stand. The controller didn't even look up.

I looked around. The walls were wood panelled – dirty with years of unwashed grime and puke and that. There was no one in there apart from me. I sat on a wooden bench fixed to one of the dirty walls and waited. My breathing was short and my stomach was turning over. I was scared and angry at the same time. The controller looked up from inside his booth, complete with bullet proof glass, and spoke into his mike.

'Where you headed for, son?'

'Just waiting for me mates,' I told him. 'Tell you when they get here.'

I thought he was going to give me a load of earache about the place not being a hangout for teenagers but he just frowned and looked away wearily.

I pulled out my phone and tried to ring Jamie but there was no signal. My phone's display read *no network*. I cussed the phone company and then moved the phone around, hoping that the signal would come back. It didn't. It was way past the two minutes that Jamie had told me he would take. At least he was bringing Reese. Reese was another mate and his entire family worked on nightclub doors. He was a great person to have on your side when shit went down, which it was about to.

I looked out of the window and watched the cars go by. A cab pulled up outside the stand and then another. Both the drivers were Asian. One a Muslim, the other a Sikh. I relaxed a bit, thinking that I'd be okay if there were drivers around. Mo wouldn't try anything in front of witnesses. But just as I was thinking that, Mo and his crew pulled up across the road and parked up. They were looking straight in at me and there were two more lads with them. I could hear the *boom, boom, boom* of the bass box in the back of their stolen car. My stomach fell. I started wishing that I had stayed in. That I had just watched telly with my sister. Now I was in trouble. Played out to a two-step beat.

I tried my phone again – nothing. I looked across the road. Mo was hanging out of the rear passenger side window. Staring in my direction. I could just about make out the dirty great scar across his cheek where Jamie had cut him. Without realising I put my hand up to *my* cheek and thought about dominoes. Ones that were put up and others that were about to be knocked down. I didn't know where Jamie and Reese were but I didn't think that I had time to wait. For some reason I decided to make a run for it. There was an alley two doors down from the cab stand, past the bookie's. If I made it down there I could jump the fence at the end and I'd be out on another street. I decided that I'd be able to lose them that way. Stupid move.

I took off out of the cab stand like a hundred-metre sprinter, hearing Mo and his gang shouting, swearing and beginning a chase. I ran to the alley, took a left into it and sprinted on, past discarded boxes. I caught one of them and rats scattered in every direction but I kept on, my chest beginning to tighten. The blood was pumping in my head and I could see the fence at the end. I hit it at full pelt and scrambled over, ripping my eighty quid jeans and my thigh on a rusty nail. Behind me I heard Mo and his crew, getting closer and closer.

Over the fence and on the adjoining street I realised my mistake. There was no one around. No cars. No people. No safety. I pulled out my phone as I ran but it was still taking the piss. *No network. No network.* I pocketed it again.

Across the road was the estate, eight low-rise blocks arranged in a rectangle around two high-rises. Concrete walkways cut between each building, leading to a square park in the centre. I headed across the road and down the nearest walkway, splashing through puddles, and crushing takeaway boxes underfoot, slipping on fried chicken bones and slimy wedges of mouldy tomato. My thigh was beginning to hurt where the rusty nail had ripped through the skin and my breathing was short and sharp. I heard the gang behind me, getting closer still.

I came out into the middle of the housing estate, into the park, which had no lighting at all. A group of three men stood by the swings, eyeing me as I ran. One of them put his hand to his mouth, spat something into it and handed it to one of the others. I skirted them, trying to gulp down air, like I'd been taught at football. In through the nose and out through the mouth. But I couldn't get enough in and my legs were beginning to cramp. Pounding steps behind me got closer and closer. Someone was right on my tail as I came out of the park area and ran towards one of the high-rises. Just get inside, I told myself. Just get inside. Lose them in the corridors.

For some reason my mum and my sister came to mind as I ran. And then I felt myself falling, as a foot swept away my trailing leg. I hit the concrete floor hard, cracking my head. A boot caught my midriff. Then another. I threw up and then the blows really began to rain in, one after the other, until I could no longer feel my legs or my arms. My head felt like it was going to explode.

Someone turned me over and sat on my chest. It was

Mo. I was drifting between reality and unconsciousness but I could still make out the sneering expression he was wearing.

'*This is for my face*,' said Mo, only the words came out as a slow, drawn out slur.

The pain shot through my stomach like fire. Like a hot needle poking at my insides. I tried to scream but nothing came. And then I felt the weight bearing down on my chest cease. Another intense stabbing pain in my midriff made me spasm. And then . . .

My mum was crying quietly when I came round. I was in a bed, in hospital. I tried to move but the pain was unbearable. There was some kind of tube down my throat and more in my arms. I couldn't move my head. My sister stood behind my mum, a grim look on her face. At the end of the bed was a man in a grey suit, with short hair and a serious expression. A copper waiting to ask me what had happened. Did I see who did it? Did I know them?

I thought about grassing up Mo. Ending it all. All that shit about vengeance. The endless cycle of stabbing and slashing. But things don't work that way. I'd get called a grass. My sister would get shit when she was out, maybe even my mum. I thought about how I could have died. But that still didn't make me tell the copper shit. It just made me angry. I looked at my mum. Looked at my sister. And put up another domino.

Johnny Too Lie

There used to be this kid that went to the same school as me, Jamie and Dal. His name was Johnny West – it probably still is. I dunno, because he kind of disappeared during Year Nine. I say disappeared but that's not exactly right. He had to do a runner because he got into some serious shit with a load of bad bwoi. And all because he couldn't stop running off his gums, lying about everything. My grandad, who lives in Jamaica, used to tell me this story when I was little, about a woman who used to carry gossip from one gate to the next, telling everyone she met the latest news. She was like a walking, talking newspaper and my grandad said that they called her 'Carry Go Bring Come'. One day the woman upset a local *rude bwoi* with her lies and she had to leave town fast.

'Jus' de shoe pon she foot an' de dress pon she *maaga* back,' my gramps had told me.

Well, when me and my friends worked out that Johnny West told lies all the time we *had* to give him a new name and that name was Johnny Too Lie. And the boy deserved it too.

I met him first hanging around down by the shops on the estate. He was on a mountain bike, trying to get in with a crew of lads, outside the off-licence. They were dissing him and he didn't even know it. I walked up and told him he had a nice bike and he grinned from ear to ear, like I'd just handed him a million quid in cash. The other lads thought he was with me and they backed off, going back to picking on the younger members of their crew. I went into the shop and got some milk for my mum and when I came out, Johnny rode back to my house with me, telling me all about his bike on the way.

'They use the same frame for the World Mountain Bike Championships,' he told me.

'*Serious?*' I asked, believing him, because I didn't know what he was like.

'Yeah, man. They change the gears and the wheels and that . . . but the frame is the same. It's this poly-carbon steel thing – you can't break it.'

'Must have cost a lot of money,' I said.

'Yeah . . . my dad got it for me – got a discount though 'cause he used to work for the company.'

We were approaching my house and I asked him if he was going to go to our school.

'Yeah – we moved here last week from America,' he told me.

'*Yeah* – which part you come from?'

'New York, man. You know – the Bronx.'

'So how come you're living here then?'

'Me dad left me mum and she grew up round here so we had to move back and that . . .'

'*Seen.* Listen, I'll check you in school tomorrow or something,' I said, as we got to my block.

'Yeah . . . cool. Later man . . .' And with that he rode off, whistling to himself.

The next time I met Johnny I was chilling out with Jamie during a lunch time. It was a few days after I'd first met him and he was walking past the tennis courts, on his own.

'Yo! Bronx *bwoi*!' I shouted at him.

'Easy, man!' he replied, grinning.

'Who's that?' Jamie asked me as Johnny walked over.

'Kid called Johnny – he's new. I seen him down the

shops on Sunday,' I said. Johnny cuffed me and nodded at Jamie.

'This is Jamie,' I told him, 'One of my best mates . . .'

'Awright,' said Johnny, turning his head to watch a couple of girls walk by.

'You like the way they look?' I asked and he grinned again.

'Yeah, man, but they *ain't* a patch on the girls in New York.'

Jamie looked confused so I cleared it up for him.

'Johnny was livin' in the Bronx until recently. His mum's from round our way though.'

'Yeah?' replied Jamie, looking unimpressed.

'So you settlin' in okay?' I asked Johnny.

'So-so . . . I ain't really made no friends yet . . .'

'Some man are funny about new kids,' I told him. 'Soon come.'

'I don't mind too much,' he told us. 'I don't need to kotch wid no crew just to fit in. Spent most of my life movin' round from one place to another . . .'

'How come?' asked Jamie.

'My dad . . . he works for some government thing.'

'I thought he worked for that bike company?' I asked, remembering our first conversation.

'That was a while ago . . . he left what he did and got a new job but it was boring and that so he went back to work for the department,' replied Johnny.

'Oh.'

'So what does he *do* then?' asked Jamie. 'Is he like a spy or something?'

'I dunno, man,' said Johnny, shrugging. 'He don't talk about it . . .'

'But he's still in New York?' I asked.

'Still living there, but he rang last night to say that he's working in Hong Kong for a month . . .'

'Yeah man – *Hong Kong* . . . Jackie Chan!' said Jamie.

'I'll get him to send me some DVDs if you like,' Johnny offered.

'What – martial arts and that?'

'Yeah – whatever . . . they're like twenty pence over there . . . Last time I went I got a *tonne* of shit.'

I looked at Jamie and whistled to show how impressed I was. Man, I'd only ever been to Jamaica, twice. Nowhere else. Not even France.

'You been Hong Kong?'

Johnny smiled and pulled out a pack of fags.

'I been *loads* of places. Hong Kong, Japan, Australia . . . nuff places, man.'

He took a fag from his pack and looked around. I didn't recognise the brand – I'd never seen it before.

'Where do people go to have a smoke?' he asked me.

'Come – mek I show you,' I told him. 'They American fags?'

'Yeah – only get 'em in New York. They're like this local brand made in the state . . . like organic and that.'

And so it went on. By the time lunch was over Johnny was one of the gang, keeping us amused with stories about the places he'd been to and what he'd got up to in the Bronx. Mad stuff about seeing crack dealers getting shot dead and serial killers being caught outside his high school. He told us about meeting members of Wu-Tung Clan and standing next to Mariah Carey in a queue. Watching Beyonce through the window of a local recording studio, when she was younger, recording her first song. And for the first year that we knew him no one really bothered to check his stories out. He was just Johnny Bronx – our interesting spar with a story for every occasion. All that changed though.

The following year, when we were in Year Eight, Johnny's stories began to get more unbelievable. Maybe because we were all a bit older and more clued up. Or maybe he just got charged up because we'd believed everything he'd said so far. Whatever. He started telling different people different stories about things. Like one time when he told Jamie and Dal that his dad was in Jamaica, working, a *day* after telling me and Misha that his old man was on a expedition in Alaska. When I had him about it he just put on that grin that he had and came up with this mad lie. He said there was *oil* under Jamaica and that his dad was learning how to drill it, *in Alaska*, so that he could pass on the secrets to the *Jamaican* government.

I went home and asked my mum about it but she just laughed at me.

'Dat bwoi too *lie!*' she told me. '*Oil?* And since *when* dem Yankee waan' 'elp de yard man?'

I could tell that she was worked up because she always lapsed into 'yard talk' when she got excited or angry. Even though she'd been born in England, my mum knew all about Jamaica. She'd lived there with her grandma from the age of six to seventeen. Her word was enough for me.

I went round to Jamie's and told him what she'd said and then we called for Dal, before going down to the recreation ground in the middle of the estate. We sat on the swings, exchanging lies that Johnny might have told us.

'He told *me*,' began Dal, 'that his parents won the New York State Lottery . . . But then they invested all the money in a dotcom company that went bust and they lost it all.'

'Whassa *dotcom*?' asked Jamie, scratching his head.

'It's an Internet company, you flea-bitten dog. Quit scratchin' like that.' said Dal.

'Piss off . . .' replied Jamie, still scratching.

'*What*? I seen a programme about American state lotteries,' I said. 'Them things are worth *millions* . . . like thirty million dollars and shit.'

'Exactly,' agreed Dal. 'That's a lotta dough to lose all of a sudden.'

'So the bwoi chats shit, man? So does everyone else,' said Jamie.

'Not me, boss,' replied Dal, shaking his head, as Misha and Tara walked up with Tara's baby brother, who was sleeping in his pushchair.

We told the girls what we were talking about and slowly they began to come up with stuff that Johnny had told them too.

'Tol' me his brother is one of them SAS soldiers,' Tara told us.

'Must work with that uncle that he's got in the CIA,'

said Misha, smiling and shaking her head.

'Man's full up of shit!' I said. 'Just wait 'til I catch up with his raas . . .'

'Call him up now,' urged Jamie. 'Let's shame him up!'

'You can't,' said Tara. 'He's away with them football trials from school.'

'*What* football trials?' I asked.

'The school ones . . . At Old Traffic or summat.'

'Old *Trafford*?' asked Jamie.

'That's what I said,' replied Tara.

'Wha'? He gonna play for Man United now an' all?' I said.

'Is that *another* lie, then?' asked Misha.

'Er . . . yeah. Just a *little* . . .' replied Jamie.

That was when Dal started to laugh out loud. Everyone turned to look at him but he just kept on laughing, his face going red and his eyes watering.

'You shot it, man?' asked Jamie. 'What the *raas* are you laughing at?'

Dal struggled to get hold of himself before he told us what was so funny.

'He tol' me that he shagged Tara . . .' he said, bursting into laughter again.

'*Ehh*!' replied Misha.

'Little bastard!' shouted Tara.

'You fuck Johnny, Tara?' I asked, knowing what her answer would be.

'*Move wid dat nastiness*! Wait 'til I catch that fool!' she shouted, her eyes blazing with anger.

'Johnny *Bronx*, my *raas*,' I said, grinning. 'Best we change that bwoi name to Johnny *Too Lie*.'

The local working girls were taking up their positions on the street corners by the time we'd finished comparing notes on Johnny Too Lie. As I made my way home with Dal we talked about getting even with him. Challenging him over his lies in public.

We didn't have to wait too long to find him but things took a different turn to what we were expecting. Big time.

It was two evenings later that me and Jamie saw Johnny. He hadn't been to school and no one had seen him around the estate. We were cooling out by the swings, watching a group of dealers doing their thing over by one of the high-rise blocks, when Johnny rode up on his bike, smiling like a nutter.

'Easy geezers!' he said, getting off and laying his bike on the ground.

'Easy,' I replied, like I didn't care one way or another.

'Got any *stories* to tell us, Johnny?' asked Jamie, before grinning at me.

'Yeah man – you know Johnny Bronx . . . nuff stories!' he replied, laughing.

'Like the one about you sleepin' wid Tara?' I said, watching his eyes dart around and his skin darken to red.

Johnny grinned.

'You know how it goes, bro . . . Just bein' one of the crew. Blaggin' and that, you get me?' he told me.

'So you never did the nasty with her?'

'Nah . . . Just winding you up.'

Jamie saw his chance and jumped in.

'What about havin' an uncle in the *CIA*, man? Or a brother in the *SAS*?'

I thought that Johnny would go even redder with the shame of being found out but he surprised me. He just stood his ground and laughed at us.

'You get pick by Man United the other day . . . at that *trial*?' added Jamie.

'Listen, man . . . I was *just*—' began Johnny.

'Just nuttin',' interrupted Jamie. 'You too lie, Johnny. We even changed yer tag man.'

'To what?' he asked.

'Johnny Too Lie,' I revealed. 'Kinda suits you . . .'

'Listen, I never meant to be *sly* . . . I was just being a geezer . . . Y'know?'

I looked at Jamie, who shrugged at me and then looked straight at Johnny.

'Is there *anythin'* that you told us that was true?'

'Yeah, man,' Johnny replied, quickly. 'Loads of it. Like, I really did live in the Bronx and my dad *does* work for the American government.'

'Just not drillin' for oil in Jamaica?' I asked.

'Er . . . No . . .' he replied, looking down at his bike.

'An' I bet you never got no love letter from Britney Spears either . . .' said Jamie.

I just shook my head. The boy was crazy. Proper wacked out. I got up off the swing I was sitting on and decided that Johnny needed a lesson. He stood where he was as I approached and he broke into a smile. A smile that disappeared when I grabbed him around the throat.

'Give us one good reason why we shouldn't kick your lyin' likkle head in?' I asked him.

His eyes were working overtime now and his face was a kind of purple colour. He looked really scared. Suddenly I felt ashamed of myself – I was twice his size and it wasn't like he had stolen anything from me. He was just a little blagger. I let him go and he fell to his knees, holding his throat and coughing. I looked at Jamie and then away. I felt really bad – like a bully – and I hate bullies. By the time Johnny got to his feet and began to speak there were tears in his eyes.

'I'm sorry . . . I'm really sorry. I never meant . . .'

'S'okay,' I said, unable to look him in the eye.

'. . . And there's this thing that I was gonna share with you and—'

He stopped as, behind us, a couple of kids on mountain bikes began to circle, like vultures waiting for their piece of the carcass. They were sniggering and pointing at Johnny, who hadn't noticed them.

'What *thing*?' demanded Jamie. 'Another of your stupid lies . . . ?'

'Nah man . . . *serious* . . . I found some shit . . .'

'What?' I asked, giving the vultures a death stare. Not that it stopped them from hanging around.

Johnny sniffed back his tears and wiped his runny nose on his sleeve like a five-year-old. Then he looked at me and Jamie and smiled a bit. Not too much but enough to say that he felt better.

'I was walking through one of them passages under the big blocks of flats,' he told us. 'And there was this *bloke* lying on the ground . . . Out cold. There was a bag next to him and I grabbed it and rode off. Thought it might be *money* . . .'

'That your *big* thing, man – telling us that you rob junkies?' asked Jamie.

'Nah . . . There's more. I went home and opened the bag and it was full of *crack*.'

'How you know it was crack?' I asked.

'I seen that shit *plenty* times in the States. My mates used to *sell it*, man!'

'*Fuck off, you knob!*' replied Jamie, disgusted at yet another lie.

'*Serious* . . . Anyway – and here's the good bit – I'm gonna sell it.'

He grinned at us again. As though he had just told us that he was going to open a newsagent's or something.

'Are you off your *head*?' I asked.

'It's easy . . . I seen all the people who hang around waiting for the dealers. That's what I've been doin' for the past few days . . . watching the crackheads . . .' he told us, like that would make it all okay and he wasn't completely out of his tiny little mind.

'An' you think that the gangs are just gonna let you do that?'

'Ain't none of their business,' he replied, trying to act brave.

Jamie got up off his swing and grabbed Johnny by his hooded top.

'That *is* them business, you likkle twat! That's what they do,' he spat at him.

'I'll share the money with you both . . .' sang Johnny, his voice pitched somewhere up near castration level.

For a *moment* me and Jamie dreamt the same dream. But *only* for a moment.

'No way. You can keep it.' I said.

'I don't want none a' dat,' agreed Jamie, letting Johnny loose.

'Don't say I didn't ask you,' he said, grabbing his bike and riding off towards the high-rises.

I looked around for the vultures but they had gone too, so I shook my head and told Jamie that I was going home. Jamie nodded and came with me.

Johnny Too Lie called my mobile about twenty times over the next two weeks and left so many text messages that I had to turn my phone off in the end. I listened to about four voice-mails and they were all the same. He kept on asking me to call him, telling me that he was in trouble and needed my help. But, just like with the boy in that story about crying wolf, he was ignored. I'd had enough of his lies and I didn't want anything to do with him at all. The boy was an idiot. A fool. And life was hard enough without having to constantly question what your so-called mate was telling you.

Besides, I'd started checking Tara, and she was still angry about the lies that Johnny had told about her, not just to me and Dal and Jamie, but all over the estate and in school too. The younger kids shouted 'slag' at her when she went to the shops and even her mum heard the rumours, which caused a whole heap of grief.

Three weeks after he'd told us about the crack, Johnny disappeared. The first rumour to go round the estate was that he had stolen a stash from one of the dealers, who had him chopped up and disposed of. The second rumour said that Johnny had sold off all the gear and skipped the country with thousands of pounds, heading back to the States to live with his dad. I didn't believe either of them, though. And with good reason.

Tara bumped into a girl from a local care home, a scraggy little thing called Jenny, who told her a very funny story. Jenny had moved to the home recently, to be reunited with her older brother, who had moved there from somewhere in Birmingham a couple of years before. Only her brother had lied about finding a stash of drugs and had done a runner when a local drug dealer believed his lies, and asked for the drugs. Her brother had refused and the dealer had threatened to kill him. He had even broken into the home and left a dead *rat* in her brother's bed.

One morning, when the care workers went to check on him, her brother was missing. The care workers asked the other kids in the home where he might have gone to, and why. Jenny told them about the drugs lie and the dealer, and they called the police who searched her brother's room. They found martial arts posters, books about New York, a torn Man United shirt, and a signed photo of Britney Spears, but no crack. They also found a diary detailing an imagined life that the boy had spent, moving around the world with his imaginary father, who just happened to work for the US government.

Johnny's still missing. No one's seen him since his trouble with the drug dealers. Tara, Misha and Jamie reckon we'll never see him again but I don't think they're right. One of these days he's gonna turn up driving some flash car, wearing *pure* gold chains and shit, and tell us a load more lies. I kind of hope he does too, because despite his lies, I kinda liked that bwoi . . .

Bhangra Boys

Bally stood outside the club and waited for his cousins. He hadn't involved himself in the fight. Now, as he stood watching the lads that Surj, Del and Pally had picked a scrap with, he hoped that they wouldn't recognise him. Not that there was much chance. He'd been standing at the bar when the trouble kicked off, like it always did when they all went out together, and as soon as the first punch had gone in, he had walked out, knowing that eventually his cousins would follow. Bally wasn't into fighting – it just didn't make any sense to him. What was the point in getting all dressed up and that, spending all that money to have a good time, just to ruin it?

The lads his cousins had fought with got into their cars and drove off and Bally relaxed a bit, enough to notice the fine looking white girl smiling at him. Her eyes were glazed over and she was wobbling slightly.

'You got a light?' she mumbled, holding out a cigarette.

'Yeah, here,' replied Bally, pulling a lighter from his jacket pocket and flicking the flame into life.

The girl took a long drag and then smiled again.

'Thanks.'

'No worries,' replied Bally, returning the smile.

There was a commotion at the door, followed by a load of swearing in Punjabi. Surj.

'Gotta go,' Bally told the girl, quickly.

'Shame . . .'

'You always come here?' he asked her.

'Sometimes. Mostly Po Na Na though . . .'

Bally's cousins were making idiots of themselves now, arguing with the head doorman, who was smiling and shaking his head.

'What night?' asked Bally, as Surj and Pally set off down the street, with Del following behind.

'Thursdays . . . Saturdays . . . want my mobile . . . ?'

He realised that there was no time and smiled again. She was fit but he had to go after the lads.

'Gotta go,' he said for the second time. 'I might see you down there one night though . . .'

'Next week – Thursday,' replied the girl, and as Bally turned to go she shouted after him. 'Don't bring them wankers though!'

Bally turned and grinned.

'No chance . . .' he told her before jogging after his cousins.

He caught up with them by a burger place. Surj was standing outside and the other two had gone in to get food. As Bally approached Surj smiled like a demented fool.

'See dat man! Run dem bwoi outta de place . . . !'

'And yourself an' all . . .' replied Bally, wondering why he had chosen a night out with them.

'Din't see you helpin' us out . . .' said Surj, accusingly.

'That's 'cause I was at the bar when it kicked off . . .' said Bally.

'Chickenshit more like . . .' countered Surj, grinning. 'Never mind – we ain't all fighters, innit . . .'

'I definitely ain't like you,' muttered Bally under his breath.

'You what?'

'Nuttin' man. What they gettin' . . . ?'

Surj looked at him like he was mad.

'Ain't gonna be no aloo gobi, is it?' he mocked.

'I might get some chips,' said Bally, ignoring him and wondering if he had enough money to get a cab home. On his own.

He walked in to find Del and Pally arguing with the Turkish bloke behind the counter.

'I *want* a *fresh* one!' shouted Del.

The Turkish bloke shrugged, said something that Bally couldn't understand and waved the kebab knife he was holding about. Instantly Bally thought of the bit from the second Fugees CD where they pretend to be in a Chinese takeaway and he grinned to himself. The bloke spoke in English.

'You want *fresh* – this *fresh* . . .'

He picked up a styrofoam container and gestured to the burger with his knife.

'That was already there when we walked in,' argued Pally.

The man shrugged and turned to another assistant behind the counter, a short, stocky man with a four inch knife scar down the left side of his face. He spoke in Turkish for about thirty seconds and then the stocky man glared at Del and Pally. He moved slowly to the counter and started to serve some of the other people in the shop.

'Oi!' shouted Pally. 'We were first . . .'

The stocky man shook his head and sighed.

'You want burger you take the one he give to you. You don't like . . . you fuck off, mate.'

Bally tried to resist but failed.

'Man, he want *beef* . . .' he said to no one in particular.

Del and Pally looked at him for a moment, not getting the joke, but behind them a couple of students started laughing and one of them called out '*flying fist of Judah!*' Bally grinned and waited for his cousins to tire of their latest argument and leave. He was hungry and he wanted a bag of chips. Not a *fight*. Not a *burger* – cold *or* hot – just a bag of chips. With a bit of mayo maybe. Only his cousins weren't in the mood to back down. Pally picked up a salt shaker and tipped its contents on the counter as Del started to throw sachets of ketchup and mayo at the men behind the counter. The short stocky one let out a low, rumbling growl, from deep inside himself somewhere. He raised his kebab knife and let out a cry, launching himself towards the flap in the counter, ready to kill.

As Bally stepped to one side, Del went white and Pally let rip a huge fart. Then they ran out of the shop, scared witless, with the kebab man chasing after them, knife glinting in the light thrown from the streetlights and neon signs. Surj, who was standing outside, doubled over with laughter, not bothering to check if the other two were okay. Bally shook his head, got his chips and joined Surj just as the kebab man was returning, red in the face and muttering in Turkish, to his shop.

'One of these days you lot are gonna get murdered, man,' Bally told Surj, who shrugged.

'Just a bit of fun, innit . . .' he replied.

'Where them two got to?' asked Bally.

'Prob'ly half way to the Punjab by now – that Paki was gonna kill 'em . . .'

Bally dropped the chip he was holding.

'He's Turkish . . .' he told Surj.

'All *muzzies* in't they . . . ?'

'You joined the BNP or something . . . ?' asked Bally, disgusted at his cousin's reply.

'I ain't no *muzzy*, man – that's all I know . . .'

For a moment Bally wanted to continue arguing but then he decided to keep quiet, eat his chips and slip away as soon as he could. As he licked a smear of mayo from one of his fingers he vowed never to go out with this particular set of cousins again. They were knobs. The sound of a bhangra ring tone broke the silence that had descended between the two. Surj flipped his phone open and spoke.

'Where you got to?' he asked. 'Round by the Rat and Parrot? You must have run fast, bro, to get round there so quick. We'll meet you outside that other bar up the street – one that plays *desi* music, innit . . .'

Surj flipped the phone shut and cuffed Bally on the back of his head.

'Come on – they's down Belvoir Street . . .' he said, walking off in the direction of the city centre.

Bally stood where he was for a moment before screwing up his chip paper and throwing it at an overflowing bin. He looked at his watch and followed Surj as a police car flew by, its sirens wailing.

The bar stood in the middle of a street lined with similar places. Up and down the road people wandered around in groups, shouting and swearing, laughing and joking. Bally stood outside the bar with the other three, waiting for the bouncer to relent and let more people in. Not that the place was busy – it wasn't. It was just the bouncer's way of making himself feel important, as he stood there with his mate, his chest puffed up, shoulders held wide. But this time Surj, Del and Pally weren't arguing. Perhaps they were scared of the doorman, or maybe they wanted to get in somewhere rather than spend the night walking round town. Eventually the five people in front of them were allowed inside and Bally got ready to flash his fake

ID at the doorman. When he ushered them through, though, the barrel-chested bouncer just gave the lads a dirty look but didn't twig that two of them, Bally and Del, were underage, and they didn't wait around for him to realise his mistake.

Inside the bar it was steamy and loud. The DJ was playing a tune by Rishi Rich which segued into a wicked Elephant Man thing. Bally watched Surj go to the bar, exchanging words with one or two people on the way, and then checked his own pockets for money. He had about seven pounds left and his cash card was at home. He decided to let Surj get the drinks as he was always loaded anyway, and put his cash away, saving it for the cab ride that he wanted to take later. One more drink, he said to himself.

'You what?' asked Pally, before stroking his goatee beard and straightening his beanie.

'Nuttin',' replied Bally, pretending that he was more interested in a couple of Asian girls dancing by a table.

'They's fit, innit?' said Del, nodding towards the girls.

'Like they's gonna touch you, *ugly bwoi* . . .' laughed Pally.

'Least I don't look *gay*,' countered Del.

'Least my *balls* has dropped, you get me?' replied Pally.

Even Bally laughed at that one, as Del kissed his teeth and told Pally to do one.

'Check a *man* at work, bwoi,' said Pally, edging towards the girls and grabbing one of them by the arm. As she turned, he whispered something in her ear. She looked at him for a moment and then turned to her friend, said something, and then the two of them walked off, giggling. Pally went bright red.

'They's just *ho*'s,' he said, trying to hide his shame.

'Oh, so ain't *fit* now then?' asked Bally, taking his drink from the returning Surj.

'Who ain't?' asked Surj, handing drinks to the other two.

'Them gal.'

'I can't see no gal,' said Surj.

'That's cause Pally got rid of 'em . . .' smiled Del.

'Ain't the first time,' laughed Surj, as Pally punched him on the arm. '*Punches* like a pussy, too.'

Some shouting went up behind them and as they turned they saw another big doorman grab hold of someone by the throat.

'Step to the side, bro!' shouted Surj, as two more doormen piled in.

Between the three of them the doormen dragged the troublemaker out of the bar, his feet catching chairs and tables on the way out. Del grinned and called the ejected drinker a wanker.

Suddenly someone threw a punch at the back of his head and he hit the ground. Surj and Pally span around and saw who had punched Del. It was a white lad, standing with two black guys and an Asian. Surj threw his glass at one of the black lads and then jumped on him, swearing in Punjabi. As Pally threw a punch, Bally took a step back, his stomach turning. The other lads looked hard and he wasn't about to get into one fight when he'd successfully avoided another earlier on. Instead he headed for the door, leaving his drink on the bar, passing the doormen heading for the trouble.

He didn't give them a second glance as he walked out into the street and up the road, heading for a taxi rank, past a crowd that was gathering in the street, one gang to each pavement, facing each other. Enough was enough and all Bally wanted to do was get a cab and go home to his bed. Only as he walked past one of the gangs, someone kicked him. When he turned, he saw the sneering face of a white lad with a shaved head.

'You want some, Abdul?' asked the white lad.

'I don't want no trouble,' replied Bally, holding up his hands. The white lad sneered again.

His head butt came from nowhere and caught Bally on the side of the head. Shocked, Bally didn't react and the lad followed up with a soft punch to the stomach. Bally jerked back, blinking, finally shielding himself.

'I said I didn't want trouble!' he shouted at the lad.

'You fuc—' began the lad, only he didn't finish his sentence because Bally caught him right under the chin with an uppercut. A lovely, controlled shot, just like he'd been taught at kickboxing.

As the white lad's legs wobbled and he hit the pavement, Bally shrugged.

'I said I din't *want* to fight, man, not that I *couldn't* . . .' he said to a couple of onlookers.

Bally dusted off his clothes and carried on up the street as he heard shouts go up and glasses being broken, and police sirens. And behind him, the patter of footsteps. He didn't turn to look but increased his own pace so that he'd get to the taxi rank quicker. He rounded a corner and walked across a concrete square, past a passage which led down to a subway. He decided to stick with the main road and he walked on, past people going in the opposite direction. He could still hear footsteps behind him but wasn't overly concerned as there were plenty of people around. But then the footsteps drew closer and someone grabbed him by the shoulder.

He span round, ready to hit whoever it was but his eyes nearly popped out of their sockets when he saw her. It was the girl from outside the club.

'Hello . . .' she said, smiling. 'I thought you'd never stop. It's murder trying to catch someone up in these shoes . . .'

Bally looked down at her feet. She was wearing impossibly high heels and her toenails were painted bright yellow. He smiled and said he was sorry.

'Thought you might be another idiot wanting a fight,' he said.

'I don't do fighting,' she replied.

'So what you doin' *here*? I thought you were at that other club . . . ?'

'I was but I only went because my friend, Priti asked me to. It was shit in there.'

'You're telling me,' said Bally.

She laughed.

'I see you got into another scrap.'

'*What?*' asked Bally.

'You've got a graze down the side of your face and there's a bruise near your temple . . .'

For some reason Bally thought of the *gurdwara* for a split second before registering what she meant. Too much to drink. He put his hand to his face. The girl reached over to put her hand on top of his. She was wearing an amazing scent, he noticed, like spices and mangoes and a hint of orange. He looked at her sparkling eyes and the way she held her hair up with artist's paint brushes. She was gorgeous.

'I didn't ask what your name is,' he said.

'You didn't take my mobile number *either* and I don't offer that to just *anyone*,' she replied, grinning.

'*So* . . . ?'

'Susie,' she said, with a flirtatious look. 'Why – you like?'

'Yeah . . .' grinned Bally.

He told her his name and said that he was on his way home only for Susie to tell him that she had other plans.

'Just a *couple* of drinks,' she urged. 'I know the guy who manages the place so we won't have to pay . . .'

'I've only got seven quid,' admitted Bally, feeling a little bit foolish. 'And I need to get home too . . .'

'Where to . . . ?' asked Susie.

'The Grange Estate . . .'

'On the A6?'

'*Yeah* . . . you know it?'

Susie took hold of Bally's hand.

'I live that way too. Tell you what – we'll get a *couple* of drinks at Po Na Na and then you can tell me *all* about yourself on the way home . . .'

'Won't be able to tell you much in a ten minute cab ride,' said Bally.

'Who said anything about a *cab*? It's a lovely night – we'll *walk* . . .'

Bally was about to complain that it would take an hour to get home but something stopped him. Something in Susie's face, in her eyes. He looked at her and smiled and totally forgot about his objection to walking.

'So this club,' he began, 'it don't play bhangra, does it?'

'No – yeah . . . well, *sometimes* . . . but don't worry, they wouldn't let your mates in . . .'

Bally smiled.

'Good, cause I've had enough of them bhangra boys for *one* night . . .'

Susie smiled at him and then put her hand on his arse.

'Good – let's go and get drunk, then.'

Bally wondered what had happened to his cousins, but only for the briefest of moments. Then he looked at Susie and smiled to himself. Why not, he thought. Why not.

She Ain't Playin'

Susie picked up her mobile, flipped it open, and smiled to herself. It was her friend, Priti.

'They call you then?' asked Priti.

'*Yeah* . . . what'd you think they'd do? Both of them – like little puppies . . .' replied Susie.

The girls giggled at each other down the line.

'*And*?' enquired Priti.

'And, I'm meeting them both at Joss's party on Friday night . . .'

There was a slight pause in the conversation before Priti spoke up.

'But what about *me*?' she asked, pretending to be hurt.

'Don't worry, sweetie – you'll be there too,' replied Susie, giggling again.

Matt watched cars drive by as he sat on a wall outside the chippy, waiting for Anil to get his lunch. The shop was full of kids from school and Anil, as usual, was stuck right at the back of the queue. Matt swore under his breath at his stupid friend before returning to thoughts of Susie, with her jet black hair, green eyes and yellow nail-polish. And that skirt. Gosh, that skirt. Just short enough to distract his attention when he sat opposite her. Just long enough to cover all her essentials.

Matt grinned to himself, got off the wall, and brushed down his expensive clothes, pushing his brown curls back on his head. He caught a glimpse of his own reflection in the chip shop window and, satisfied that he looked as handsome as ever, he grinned again. A couple of girls on the other side of the glass smiled at him but he ignored them. Jenny Cole. Done her, as the more uncouth chaps at school would say. Jessie Martin. Same. And as for Holly . . . well everyone had been there he thought, as he looked at his expensive watch, that his father had brought back from a trip to Switzerland. He walked to the door and told Anil to hurry up.

'Yeah, yeah,' replied Anil, grinning because he was pushed up against Holly Sandhu in the crush.

'You *mind*?' spat Holly, pushing him away.

'Don't mind me,' replied Anil, 'It's not my fault. The shop's *rammed*.' He emphasised the word 'rammed' in the way that some of the other boys did. The ones that came from lesser families and spoke in 'street' language. Even as he'd said it, he'd thought that it hadn't sat right. It just wasn't the way he spoke.

'Just get the fuck off,' Holly told him.

Some of the younger kids giggled at Holly's foul language as Anil decided to back off a bit. There were much better girls to get close to in the upper school anyway, he thought, as he ordered his chips. Like Susie . . .

Matt and Anil had made the bet a few months earlier. They were the undisputed kings of pulling girls at the upper school. Not that it was particularly difficult. They were both from rich families and always had the best clothes, carried the best mobile phones and could afford to buy their latest conquests anything they wanted. The girls fell at their feet like leaves in autumn. The other lads envied them. Good looks and popularity. It was what had driven the two of them together. Matt, captain of the rugby team, in the gym every day, honing a six pack. Anil, the best footballer in the school, light-skinned with emerald eyes. Together they had copped off with all the best-looking girls, often the same ones. Occasionally at the same parties. Heavyweight ladies champions, like some of the other boys said . . .

But Susie was different. She'd turned up at the upper school halfway through their GCSEs, wearing a paint brush in her hair, to hold it up, and a yellow mini skirt, with bright yellow nail-polish. Striking and different. Like a breath of fresh air. A new girl. A new mission. Only things were much harder than either Matt or Anil had expected. Susie smiled, flirted and occasionally made suggestive comments but neither of the lads had been able to get as much as a number from her for a few months. Susie had brushed off their advances, one by one. She was always busy with her friends or out with her family. Doing her schoolwork or writing her first novel. Matt had started to call her 'Miss Unobtainable'. And Anil had decided one day that she was worthy of a bet – a challenge for both of the lads. A way of proving, once and for all, who was the number one when it came to the ladies.

'Fifty pounds?' Anil had suggested, as they sat in the library at school, a few months earlier.

'It's not enough,' Matt had replied, brushing the suggestion off. 'I won a hundred pounds just for getting Jenny Cole before you did . . .'

'How much you got in mind then?' asked Anil.

'Something that reflects the extra special attentions we'll have to pay her . . .'

'*Two* hundred pounds?' offered Anil.

'That's better . . .' laughed Matt.

'I hope she's worth it,' said Anil.

'It's a wager,' replied Matt. 'The wager is always the most important thing.'

'*Winning* is the most important thing,' said Anil, repeating a mantra his father used.

'Of course it is.' Matt smiled. 'Of *course* it is . . .'

The first one of them to try had been Matt, a week or so after they had made their bet. He had followed Susie home, to find out where she lived, in order to send her chocolates and flowers. Thinking that she hadn't noticed him following behind, Matt had hidden around the corner, behind a hedge. Yet able to see into the house. Susie had appeared at a first floor window, in her bra, ten minutes after going inside, and Matt could have sworn that she had looked right at him, hidden as he was, and smiled. It had been enough to make him retreat. The following day he'd ordered expensive chocolates and a huge bouquet of flowers and had them delivered to her house, telling Anil about her appearance at the window.

The day after the flowers had been delivered, Matt and Anil had been sitting in the common room when Susie and two of her friends sat down behind them.

'It's amazing, isn't it,' laughed Jenna, one of Susie's friends, as Matt and Anil strained to listen.

'Flowers and chocolates,' said Susie, shaking her head. 'How original.'

Anil shot Matt a look and half of a smile. Matt glowered.

'Was it the same pervert that was watching you at your window?' asked Jenna.

'Most likely,' replied Susie, smiling at Jenna and Priti. 'Couldn't see him properly, though.'

'How disgusting . . .' said Priti.

'Well whoever it was,' Susie said, a little louder. 'This young lady ain't playin'.'

'Was the card that came with the flowers signed?' asked Jenna.

'No – just the initial '*M*',' laughed Susie.

'Sad sack,' giggled Priti.

The girls giggled some more and then left to go to their next lesson.

'First round to the young lady,' smiled Anil as he watched Susie walk away.

'Let's see what you have to offer shall we?' replied Matt, trying to look unfazed.

A few days later, Saturday, Susie woke up and went downstairs to find a letter addressed to her. The writing was unfamiliar and when she opened the envelope two tickets fell out. She picked them up and looked at them. Tickets for The Royal Shakespeare Company at Stratford. The most expensive seats for a production of Romeo and Juliet, opening night, complete with invitations to the champagne reception with the cast afterwards. There was also a letter, signed 'from an admirer', in which she was asked to call a mobile number to confirm that she would attend. She walked over to the telephone and dialled the number. It went straight through to the answering service. Susie cleared her throat and thanked the mystery ticket sender. It was her parents' anniversary and she would be passing the tickets on to them, as a present. She thanked whoever it was once again and put the phone down, smiling to herself.

At school the following Monday she giggled about it with Priti, just within earshot of Anil and Matt. Matt grinned from ear to ear and told Anil that he hoped that the tickets hadn't cost him too much.

'Nothing, actually,' replied Anil. 'My father got them through one of the businesses. He was the caterer so they were free.'

'Now, I don't *think* that counts,' suggested Matt.

'Just using my initiative,' replied Anil.

'Clever of you to know that it was her parents' wedding anniversary . . .' laughed Matt.

Anil swore at his friend.

Things continued this way for a few months, with each of the lads trying a number of different things, none of which seemed to work. Whenever they spoke to Susie she was polite – flirtatious even – but she gave nothing away. Nothing to suggest that she would give in to one of them. It was a game, and she was playing. Only she wasn't playing their game. She was playing her own. She knew *all* about Matt and Anil. She had known all along. It wasn't exactly hard to work out, what with their arrogant posturing and flash clothes, and she *had* been warned about the two lads when she'd first arrived at the upper school.

'Big-headed, pampered wankers,' Priti had said. 'Think

they can have anything or anyone they want because their daddies are rich.'

'Met their type before . . .' Susie had replied, smiling.

'They even took *pictures* of one girl, Holly Stevens, in her underwear, after she got off with Matt. Got her drunk at a party. They showed the photos to all the lads they play sports with,' added Priti.

'That's *disgusting* – poor Holly. Didn't anyone have them about it?' asked Susie.

'No – they think they're untouchable. God, just imagine what they'll be like when they're older . . .'

'Just like their *daddies*, no doubt,' Susie had replied.

'Someone needs to teach those two a lesson,' Priti had said, planting the seed of an idea in Susie's mind.

'*Yes*,' she'd said, pulling out her mobile phone. 'When is Joss having her party again . . . ?'

Anil looked at his mobile phone in disbelief. He read the sender's name for the fifth time and then re-read the message.

Joss prty. fri nite. c u deh sxy. Suz. Xxx.

He tossed his chip wrapper to the floor and looked up for his friend, Matt. He was tempted to show him Susie's message but decided he shouldn't. What a way to win their bet, he thought. Not telling his friend anything of this new development and then surprising him at the party. Imagine the look on his face. It would be perfect. He'd get the money, the kudos *and* the girl and Matt would have to bow down to *his* superiority with the ladies. As he made his way back to school, walking some way behind Matt, who was too busy chatting up some common-looking girl to notice, his phone bleeped at him twice. Another message. He glanced up and saw Matt taking out his own phone, smiling at his best friend's unerring ability to glean phone numbers from girls, even ones like the girl he was talking to. He looked at the new message.

Hope u is UP 4 it. u r so sxy. Suz.xxx.

Anil's heart missed a beat. His face broke into an uncontrolled smile. He was *IN*. Big time. He saved her message and put his phone away, smiling to himself for the rest of the afternoon. After school, Matt's father picked them both up in his Aston Martin, and as they pulled away from the school gates, amidst gasps of admiration and glances of envy, Anil mentioned the party the following Friday night.

'Should be good,' replied Matt.

'And I suppose the wager still stands?' asked Anil.

'Wager? Are you boys competing again?' asked Matt's father with a smile.

'Just a little bet,' Matt told him.

'You know, your father and I have a little flutter on the golf course now and then,' Matt's father told Anil.

'Daddy mentions it from time to time,' replied Anil.

'Bugger always wins too,' laughed Matt's father, cutting in front of a woman in a Golf GTI. 'Bloody woman in her jumped up shopping trolley!'

Matt and Anil grinned as the Aston purred through the gears.

Matt and Anil arrived at the party just after nine, both of them with fresh haircuts and new clothes, immaculately presented.

'Hey *boys* . . .' giggled Joss as she led them into the crowded house.

'We bought some booze,' offered Matt, nodding towards Anil.

'Yeah – some beers and a bottle of Jack Daniels,' said Anil.

'How lovely . . .' replied the slightly drunken host.

Joss took the bag Anil was holding from him and disappeared into the living room. Matt shrugged and walked into the kitchen, pushing through a crowd of people.

'Lot of people here,' observed Anil, looking around for Susie. Loud dance music was making the walls throb.

'Indeed – some of them smoking the old *wacky baccy* too,' said Matt, smiling.

Anil opened the huge fridge and pulled out two bottles of lager which he opened with his Swiss Army knife, handing one to Matt.

'Cheers Anil.'

'So you got anyone in mind?' asked Anil.

Matt shrugged. 'Obviously there's the bet to consider but the young lady doesn't seem to be around at the moment . . .'

He looked over to the entrance to the garden room which led on into a pool room. There were two girls from the year below them standing by the door with drinks. Matt smiled and ran a hand through his hair.

'. . . So I think I'll say hello to those two.'

Anil smiled. With Matt busy chatting to the girls in the kitchen he had ample time to find Susie.

'I think I'll go and explore the house,' said Anil, matter-of-factly . . .'

'Cool,' replied Matt, watching his friend leave the

kitchen. He pulled out his mobile and scrolled through the text messages he'd received until he arrived at the latest one from Susie. He smiled. His friend had *no* idea . . .

Anil stood at the entrance to the living room, watching some of the younger revellers dancing. Others stood around smoking and drinking and in the middle of the crowd Joss was pulling on a home-made bong, the water bubbling visibly. She passed it to a couple of older lads that Anil didn't recognise, and they both took their turns. Anil made a mental note to approach the lads later. They seemed like the types who'd have a little gear to sell. He turned and wandered across the hallway to another couple of rooms. One was full of people from school, playing drinking games with tequila, and the other seemed to be full of couples molesting each other, in every available corner. There was even a couple on the dining table. Anil searched the second room for Susie but couldn't see her. Instead he watched Mitesh Chandra, a lad from his school, trying to remove some girl's bra with one hand. He shook his head and smiled to himself. No class. He turned and thought about exploring the upper part of the house, wandering if Matt had managed to pull yet. As he left the 'copping off' room he turned to find Susie's friend, Priti, standing next to him.

'Hello,' grinned Priti.

'Hi . . .' replied Anil, looking past her for Susie.

'Susie is a bit tied up at the moment but she asked me to take *care* of you,' Priti told him.

Anil raised an eyebrow.

'Don't worry,' reassured Priti, 'she's just getting herself ready for you.'

As Susie's friend winked at Anil he didn't know what to say. Instead he pulled out a packet of Marlboros and offered one to Priti.

'*Ooh* thanks, Anil, but don't tell my mother . . .' said Priti, accepting his offer of a light and trying hard not to laugh.

'My pleasure,' replied Anil, smiling.

'Let's have a few shooters,' suggested Priti.

Why not, thought Anil, as he followed her into a side room, brushing past Holly Sandhu who was on her way out. The two girls smiled at each other as another one of Susie's friends, Jenna, offered Anil a shot of whisky. He took it and downed it in one, just in time for Jenna to pass him another . . .

* * *

Matt watched Susie down her shots of whiskey as though it was water, one after the other. Not wanting to seem inexperienced Matt followed suit, hoping that his face didn't betray the burning sensation he was feeling in his throat and belly. But Susie didn't seem to notice, as she poured another round of shots and took a long drag on the spliff, that Holly Sandhu had just brought into the pool room. Matt's attention settled on the curve of Susie's breasts as they sat proudly in her bikini top and he stirred a little, glad that he had stocked up on condoms earlier.

'Here we go again,' giggled Susie, running a finger from her neck to the deep well of her cleavage. Matt's eyes followed the route that Susie's finger took as Holly Sandhu giggled in the background.

'Holly – let Matt have some of that spliff will you,' asked Susie, handing him another shot of whisky. Matt downed it in one.

'Here you go, Matthew,' said Holly handing him a fresh one and lighting it for him.

Matt inhaled deeply and then handed it back to Susie who shook her head.

'That's yours, Matt,' she told him, leaning forward and trying not to laugh. 'I've got my own, too . . .' she said, holding a half-smoked joint in her hands.

'Cool,' replied Matt, trying not to slur his words.

He hadn't bargained on Susie being such a party animal but it made her seem more attractive somehow. As Matt sat back he wondered how Anil was getting on, and smiled at the thought of the two hundred pounds that would soon be heading his way. He saw some other girls join Susie and Holly by the pool. The other Holly, Holly Stevens, and Jenny Cole too. His head began to swim as he tried to remember what the connection between the girls was as they stripped down to their bikinis . . .

Anil lay back on a bed about two hours later and watched the room spin as Priti and Jenna removed his clothes. He hadn't bargained on this but Anil wasn't a man who was going to complain when lady luck smiled down. He heard a knock at the door and then Susie walked in with a huge smile spread across her face.

'You've started without me,' she purred as her friends giggled. She looked down at Anil, slowly unbuttoning her shirt, her hair damp. Anil smiled, tried to say something and then closed his eyes as Susie sat astride him. He thought of the look on Matt's face and the money that would soon be his. His stomach turned suddenly and he fought back the urge to retch. It just wouldn't do to seem a lightweight in the present company. Just wouldn't do at all. But then the room suddenly became much darker, as someone else entered. Anil fought to keep his eyes open but eventually he lost consciousness and slipped into a dreamy sleep . . .

The group e-mail that went round the upper school's intranet the following week was bad enough, with its semi-explicit pictures of Anil and Matt handcuffed to each other, naked, but it was the posters that really took the biscuit. That task had been left to Holly Stevens and her new boyfriend, Karam, at Susie's request. By mid-morning on the Wednesday outraged locals were pulling down the posters all over town. They were even found underneath the frozen peas at Asda and slotted in with the advertising junk mail that accompanied the local free paper, right there next to offers for blinds and interest-free sofas. By the time that the principal of the school had demanded an explanation at Friday's assembly, the poor lads who were the centre of attention had moved quietly on to A-level colleges in the city, a situation hastened no doubt by the discovery of Polaroids of Matt and Anil taped to their fathers' cars, as the proud parents had been playing a round or two of golf.

Everyone involved in the sting, from the two Hollys through to the lads drafted in by Joss, stayed quiet and the following week there was a small news item covering the scandal in the free paper, seven or eight lines of copy about falling moral standards and lax discipline in schools, all written by the local vicar. As Joss, Holly Stevens, Priti and Susie sat reading it in the common room, they smiled at each other . . .

Carnival Day

Tara woke up to the sound of loud reggae music thumping through the bedroom wall, and to bright, warm sunshine filtering through her curtains. The music was coming from her mum's bedroom, a bass heavy tune about beating down Babylon. She looked around for a moment, trying to work out what day it was and saw a pair of boxer shorts on the floor, lying next to Rizla™ papers and a quart bottle of vodka. Reese had obviously forgotten his underwear on his way out, tiptoeing through the flat at five in the morning. She rolled over, gathered up her duvet and smiled to herself. She'd fancied that boy all the way through school and finally she'd caught him. And then she remembered what day it was. Carnival day.

An hour later Tara was making breakfast for her brother and sister. The baby, Harvey, was still with her mum, but Henry, who was three, and Shannon, seven, were sitting watching Saturday morning telly and waiting for their food. As she waited for the eggs to soft boil, Tara cut slices of toast into soldiers and wondered what she was going to wear later. She decided to give Misha a call, provided her friend had managed to get out of bed. She recalled leaving Misha and Dal arguing outside some club in town about some stupid little thing or other, as she and Reese had grabbed a lift with Jamie and David. There'd been some trouble in the club but she couldn't remember what exactly, only that Charlie had been kicked out with blood pouring from his head and that Mo and his crew had been in there. She shook her head as she thought about the ongoing feud between her friends and Mo's gang, hoping that Charlie hadn't been too badly hurt.

'Tara-rah, where's my breakfast!' shouted Shannon from the living room.

'It's comin' you little witch! Just hush yuh mout'!' Tara shouted back, before pouring herself some juice.

The reggae music was still shaking the flat when she sat down with Henry and Shannon to eat. Her mum was a big time reggae fan anyway but Carnival day was different. The local community station played revival tunes all morning and Tara smiled as she remembered being five years old and singing along to the same tunes she could hear now, with her mum making up new words.

She could remember all the artists too – Horace Andy, Cocoa Tea, Garnett Silk, the Mighty Diamonds – loads of them. Over the years, Tara had become more of a garage and R'n'B fan but she loved reggae the same way she had when she had been young. And on Carnival day it was everywhere.

'Who was that leaving in the middle of the night?' asked Shannon.

Tara felt herself blush but she kept her cool.

'What you on about, Shan?' she asked.

'I was in the loo because I couldn't *sleep* and I needed to *pee* and I *would* have wet myself and so I went . . .'

'Take a breath, sis,' grinned Tara. Her sister often spoke without pausing, sometimes so much so that she would find herself out of breath at the end of her sentences.

'. . . and there was a *man* and he was like mummy's boyfriend and your daddy Tara-rah 'cos he was *black* and he was leaving *our* house and he was carryin' clothes and he was . . . *and* . . . *and* . . .'

Shannon stopped to take a deep breath but didn't continue because their mum walked through the door with her boyfriend, Marcus, in tow.

'You get them their breakfast, Tara?' yawned her mum.

'No – these little pink space mummies came down and

they bought it with them,' replied Tara, before returning her gaze to the TV.

'And who was in your room last night . . . ?'

Tara swallowed hard.

'*No one* . . . just Reese. He walked me back and then we had a drink and he left . . . *why*?'

Tara's mum looked at her boyfriend and winked.

'Think I've hit a nerve there, Marcus,' she said.

Marcus sat down between Henry and Shannon, ruffling Henry's hair.

'Innit . . .' he said, smiling and yawning at the same time.

'See I *told* you. I told you that there was a *man* in the house and he was like mummy's *boyfriend* . . . !' said Shannon.

'Poo!' said Henry with a grin, pointing at the TV screen, where Justin Timberlake was dancing in his latest video.

'Dis likkle man 'ave some taste,' laughed Marcus, as they all cracked up.

'Too right,' said Tara, 'I can't see all the fuss – the bwoi too ugly . . .'

'Well *I* think he's *cute*,' defended Shannon, looking slightly sad. 'And so does Parvinder *and* Simran *and*

Geeta at my school *and* Miss Patel only she can't fancy him cos she's havin' a man from *India* come to here to *marry* her and make her his *flushing bride* . . .'

'You mean *blushing* . . .' corrected Tara.

'That's what I *said* and . . .'

'OK, OK,' interrupted their mother. 'That's enough. Eat your breakfast, Shan, and then get in the bath – we've gotta go in town before we go up carnival.'

Tara shot her mum a look.

'Not you . . . you can do what you like,' replied her mum, 'but I need you to take Henry with you until I get up to the park about four . . .'

'MUM . . . !'

'Come on Tara – it's only until four and it ain't like he's gonna tell me what you get up to . . .' argued her mum.

Tara looked at her brother who was now dipping a little finger into the soft egg yolk and smearing it around an ear.

'OK . . . but just until four . . . if I don't see you by then I'm gonna sell him . . .'

'Thanks, baby,' smiled her mum, grabbing a tissue to wipe Henry's hands.

'Ain't like I don't look after them all the time anyway . . .' replied Tara.

'Don't get cheeky, Tara . . . I know you're gonna ask me for money later so just play the game . . .'

Tara looked at Marcus.

'Don't look at me,' he said, shrugging. 'I'm on duty later . . . the Chief Constable wants all the black coppers down the park for the newspapers . . .'

Tara shook her head.

'Dunno *how* you can do that . . .' she told him in disgust.

'Is a livin' sister,' replied Marcus. 'Is where else a black man get paid *that* kind of money round *here*?'

'Babylon . . .' grinned Tara.

Marcus grinned back. '*Leave* it . . . and lay off the spliffs later or I'll have to arrest you . . .'

'Yuh can try, *bacon bwoi* . . .' replied Tara, jumping up from her seat and heading for the kitchen.

'Cheeky little . . .' began Marcus, just as Henry shoved the remains of his egg into his face.

Once Tara and Misha had decided what to wear they dressed Henry and the three of them met up with the gang outside Dal's, where he was waiting with Jamie and David. David's car stereo was pumping out a Beenie Man CD and Tara could smell the sweet perfume of weed floating in the cool breeze. She looked at David and seeing the grin on his face, worked out who had the ganja.

'You mash-up already?' she asked him, holding on to Henry so that he wouldn't run away. The little boy struggled and made whinging noises but Tara had him in a firm grip.

David shrugged and carried on smiling but didn't reply. Jamie gave Tara a funny look before asking her where Reese was.

'Dunno – he left mine late . . .' replied Tara, looking at Misha rather than Jamie.

'So you and him get it on . . . ?' asked Jamie.

'None of your business, bwoi,' said Tara, pulling Henry back.

Jamie grinned. 'Check you out . . . first you did Johnny Too Lie and now it's Reese,' he said.

'You know I never touched that dutty likkle bwoi . . .' replied Tara quickly.

'Rest yuhself, man,' said Dal. 'He's only takin' the piss . . .'

'Yeah, well . . .'

An Audi A6 with blacked out windows drove past slowly, the bass bins vibrating, as David and Jamie looked on in envy and Henry gurgled.

'Gonna get me one of them,' said David.

'Yeah and I'm gonna win the lottery,' replied Jamie.

'Who's that?' asked Misha, as the car disappeared round the corner.

'Dunno,' replied Tara, watching Henry as he stooped to pick up a stone.

'What you doin' you likkle monkey?' she asked him.

Henry took the stone and threw it at David's car.

'*Oi!*' shouted Jamie. 'Leave the car alone, my yout' . . .'

Henry looked at his big sister and thought about crying but instead he smiled and said 'poo' to Jamie.

'You got him all day?' Misha asked, grabbing Henry's head and shaking him gently.

'Just till four. Mum's meeting me up at the park.'

'*Gutted* . . .' laughed Dal.

'He's my brother – what was I gonna say – *no* . . . ?'

'She still seein' that Marcus?' asked Misha.

'Yeah . . .'

'What, that *copper*?' asked Jamie.

'Yeah, him. He's okay really . . .'

'Rather you than me,' replied Jamie.

'Well that's cos I ain't a *t'ief* like you,' Tara reminded him.

They carried on talking for a while before David drove

them all to the park. Once there, the lads went off to get drinks and Tara and Misha found a spot on the grass where there weren't too many people. The park was packed already and the smell of barbecued jerk chicken and fried fish was making Tara's stomach rumble.

Henry was running round after a Staffordshire Bull Terrier that belonged to a couple who lived across the way from Tara. The dog was nudging Henry with its head and Henry giggled each time. A couple of other kids joined in, one of them holding a balloon that Henry wanted. Tara looked on as Henry grabbed the kid with the balloon and tried to take hold of the string. The kid tried to push Henry away but he stood his ground, with the dog running rings around them. Suddenly the other kid let go of the string and the balloon soared quickly into the sky, buffeted by the breeze. The kid began to cry and Henry, sensing that he might get told off, ran towards Tara with his arms open. Tara grabbed him and laughed.

'Idiot bwoi,' she said softly, pinching his nose lightly.

Henry pushed her away and ran off once more.

'He's nuts,' said Misha.

'Yeah . . . takes after his mum,' agreed Tara.

'So, where's Reese?' said Misha, changing the subject.

'Couldn't tell you . . .'

'You tie him up and leave him in yer bed?' asked Misha before grinning suggestively.

'Yeah wid his hairy ass on show to the world . . .' laughed Tara.

'So what a gwaan?' Misha was pushing for details and Tara realised that she wouldn't stop until she got them. She sighed and gave Misha what she wanted – in full colour detail.

When the lads returned with Reese in tow, they found the two girls rolling around on the grass in hysterics.

'What's so funny?' asked Dal, as Misha grabbed his leg and tried to stop herself from crying.

'Nuttin' . . .' replied Tara, with a straight face when she saw Reese. She didn't want him to think that she was mad.

Misha wiped the tears away and sat up, brushing grass from her clothes. 'What'd you get me?' she asked Dal.

Dal handed her two Bacardi Breezers, one of which she gave to Tara.

'Gee, thanks baby . . .' Tara said in a mock New York accent.

The lads sat down and began to talk about the night before, wondering if Charlie was okay, as Tara shot Reese a smile every now and then. The sun was blazing and behind them Aba-Shanti sound system was stringing up its speaker cables and power lines. It took about half an hour before the man that ran the sound dropped a needle on his first tune. As the rhythm of *Shine Eye Gal* by Black Uhuru began to filter through the giant speaker boxes, she took a swig of her drink and shut her eyes, letting the warmth and the vibes take over. Carnival day was the lick . . .

It was gone two in the afternoon when Tara realised that Henry wasn't with them any more. She looked around frantically, trying to spot her brother in the crowds, but every time she saw a kid that resembled Henry from behind, it turned out to be someone else. Something in her stomach clenched tight like a vice and she nearly cried out, holding it back at the final moment. She turned to Reese, who sitting beside her, holding a big spliff.

'Have you seen Henry?' she asked, urgently.

Reese smiled and said that Henry had been with Jamie the last time he had seen him. Tara asked Jamie, who was standing talking to a couple of older lads from the estate. When Jamie didn't reply, Tara's voice rose.

'Jamie – where's my brother?' she asked again.

This time Jamie heard her.

'He was round here somewhere . . . I think Misha and Dal had him. What's up?'

'I've lost him . . .' admitted Tara. 'I thought he was here but I can't see him.'

Reese picked up the panic in her voice and handed his spliff to Charlie, who had joined them earlier.

'Come,' he said, commandingly. 'Let's go find Misha . . . I'm sure she was holding him . . .'

Tara looked uncertain.

'But you said you seen him with Jamie last . . .'

'And then Misha . . . I *think* . . .'

Tara's face dropped.

'Oh shit,' she said, quietly.

'Come on,' said Reese, getting up and pulling her up too.

Reese got out his mobile and rang Misha's number. The phone must have rung once before Misha answered it.

'You got Henry?' asked Reese, immediately.

Tara couldn't make out what Misha was saying, even though she had placed her ear almost next to Reese's head.

'When . . . ?' she heard Reese ask.

There were more faint words that she didn't understand before Reese swore.

'WHAT?' asked Tara, sensing that things were wrong.

'He ain't with them,' Reese told her.

'Oh no . . .'

Behind them a siren pierced the air as the sound man dropped a fresh tune, a thundering dub cut of Bob Marley's *Crazy Baldhead*. But Tara wasn't listening. Her mind was running through too many scenarios about where Henry could have got to. None of them were particularly comforting. She turned to Reese with tears in her eyes.

'I'm gonna get murdered by Mum,' she said, feeling a chill run down her back despite the heat of the day.

Reese put an arm around her and said that it would be OK.

'We'll get the crew together and look for him,' he said. 'He's gotta be on the park somewhere. We'll find him.'

Tara began to scout the area around Aba-Shanti sound as Reese got the others together. One by one, all of her friends began to gather at the sound. They decided to split up and search different parts of the park. There were a lot of people around and Tara didn't feel confident. What if Henry had run out towards the main road and been run over? What if someone had taken him? She shuddered at the thought.

'Right,' said Reese. 'We're gonna check out the food stalls and the fun fair . . . he might have wandered over there.'

'But what if some nasty . . . ?' Tara began to say.

'Don't think like that,' replied Reese. 'We gotta be positive . . . It's carnival, man. Someone will pick him up and take him to the police tent . . . ain't gonna be no nonces on the park today.'

They walked quickly to the middle of the carnival where there were stalls selling everything from fried plantain to samosas and coconuts. The smell of food was everywhere but Tara had forgotten about her hunger. She started at the first stall she came to and searched every face and every corner, trying to spot Henry. There were so many young children that her task was almost impossible, and nearly an hour of searching, doubling back on herself and asking strangers if they had seen Henry, led to nothing. She found herself standing back at the first stall she had searched, with a hot and worried Reese, looking at her watch. It was nearly half-past three and she had to meet her mum by Aba-Shanti at four, *with* her brother.

Reese rang round the rest of the gang and came up with nothing. None of them had seen Henry and they had been everywhere. Charlie and Anisha had even walked halfway into the city centre, through the returning carnival floats, all to no avail.

'No one's seen him,' he told Tara.

'*What am I gonna do*?' replied Tara, crying openly now.

'We're gonna have to go to the police tent . . .' said Reese.

'But Marcus will be there,' said Tara. 'He'll tell my mum . . .'

'We ain't got a choice, Tara. Yer mum's gonna find out anyway . . . come on, we have to tell them. Henry ain't nowhere . . .'

Tara thought about continuing her search but realised quickly that Reese was right. The longer they left it, the more likely it was that Henry wouldn't be found. It had been more than an hour and a half since she had found out he was missing. She looked at Reese and broke down. Reese grabbed her and held tight to her, trying to calm her down, as passers-by stopped to ask what was wrong. Reese told them that he had it under control and led Tara towards the police tent.

Marcus called his colleagues immediately once Reese

told him about Henry. When he'd finished on his walkie-talkie he turned to Tara and gave her a hug.

'Come on,' he said, 'let's go and find him.'

'But we've been looking for ages,' Tara told him. '. . . And it's no good. We can't find him anywhere . . .'

'Do you know how many lost kids I dealt with last year?' he asked her.

When Tara didn't reply he told her that it was eleven.

'Kids wander off. They get excited by all the bright colours and the lovely smells and then they turn up . . .'

'But he ain't anywhere . . .' repeated Tara. 'Mum's gonna kill me . . .'

'Where did you say you'd meet her?' asked Marcus.

'By Shanti,' Reese told him. 'In about three minutes . . .'

Tara panicked again and tried to run for the exit but Reese grabbed her and held on.

'Come on,' he said. 'It'll be okay, baby. All of dem babylon are looking for him.'

Marcus gave him a stern look and Reese apologised.

'Sorry . . . I mean *police*,' he said, correcting himself.

The walkie-talkie crackled and a voice asked for Marcus to 'come in'.

Marcus told Reese to take Tara over to her mother and

said he would follow them in a moment. As he watched them walk off, he replied to the call. He could hear the thumping bass of a sound system playing R'n'B as he listened. And then suddenly he said 'oh shit' and shoved his radio back in its pouch. He stood and thought hard for a moment and then he ran as fast as he could . . .

Tara and Reese saw Marcus as he flashed past them, weaving quickly through the crowds.

'Oh fuck . . . !' shouted Reese, setting off after him.

Tara stood where she was for a moment. A sinking feeling took hold of her and her stomach turned sickeningly. Something had happened. Something bad. She started to run but people kept on getting in her way and a couple of times she nearly collided with food stalls as she made her way after the other two. The sirens blaring from the sound system grew closer as she tried to stop herself from crying. All she could think about was Henry. As she approached Aba-Shanti's pitch, she was nearly hysterical. She searched the crowd for her mum, spotting Reese over by the sound system's stall, where they were selling live CDs and vinyl. She pushed her way through the people in front of her and saw her mum, standing with Reese's aunt and a couple of other women, all of them swaying to the heavy bassline. The sound was so powerful that Tara's ribcage vibrated and she thought that she might be sick.

As she approached she saw her mum look up, a can of lager in her hands. Her mum's face was searching, looking for Henry, who obviously wasn't with Tara.

'Where's your brother?' she shouted above the music.

Tara felt her knees go weak and her heart miss a beat. She looked to Reese for help but realised that it was up to her to tell her mum that Henry was gone.

'He's—' she began but she was cut short by Marcus who appeared next to her suddenly. Holding Henry . . .

'He's with me!' shouted Marcus.

Tara watched her mum's expression change from questioning to satisfied. Then Marcus smiled and told Tara that he'd sort it out with her mum. Say that *he'd* been with Henry. She heard Henry giggle and say 'poo' and then she passed out . . .

The sound system was playing one of its own tunes, *Tear Down Babylon*, when Marcus walked over to Tara and her friends. As he sat down, Tara noticed Jamie and David drift away, looking worried and hiding their spliff.

'You okay?' asked Marcus, ignoring the strong smell of ganja.

'Yeah . . .' replied Tara, looking relieved.

'Your mum thinks that you were pissed . . . that's why you passed out. She doesn't know that Henry went missing and I ain't gonna tell her . . .' he said.

'Thanks Marcus,' Tara said, smiling for the first time since Henry had been found. 'Where was he anyway?'

Marcus grinned. 'One of Shanti's crew found him wandering in and out of the crowd. He picked him up and was talking to his girlfriend when one of my colleagues approached him. He was just about to take Henry over to the tent . . .'

'I can't believe I let him out of my sight . . .' said Tara.

'Nuh worry yuhself. It happens . . .' Marcus told her.

'Thank you for not telling Mum,' Tara repeated.

'No worries,' smiled Marcus. 'Just don't do it again.'

Reese approached with drinks and sat down, holding a spliff. He didn't even register that Marcus was there.

'Shit . . . sorry,' apologised Tara, grabbing the spliff and hoping that Marcus wouldn't go mad.

'You have a burn on dat ting fe mi?' asked Marcus, looking around.

Reese gave him a funny look and then shook his head,

smiling as Marcus took the spliff from Tara and took a crafty drag, blowing the smoke down into the ground. He handed it back to Tara and stood up.

'Best get back to work,' he said with a wink.

'Nah, man . . . mi nevah see Babylon bwoi wid a spliff . . .' said Reese.

'Is carnival day, my yout',' replied Marcus. 'Res' yuhself . . .'

Tara watched him walk away with a big grin on her face. He was cool, she thought. For a copper . . .

Bhangra Girls

You like that school then?' Jaspal, who preferred her nickname of Jazz, asked her cousin.

Dee smiled at her and nodded.

'It's cool, Jazz. There's loads of *apne* guys and that . . .'

'Eh – watch you, man! . . . Checkin' out the Asian guys.'

Dee smiled.

'Don't tell me you don't do the same at your school.'

Jazz watched as her cousin readjusted her new Punjabi suit, wondering where she had got it. No doubt some shop down the Soho Road in Handsworth where Dee, whose real name was Daljit, lived with her family. The top was Thai style, with a round neck and intricate embroidery and backless; *very* daring for a Punjabi wedding. The trousers were boot cut and tight around the bum, showing off her cousin's shape to perfection. Jazz wished she had bought something similar, not that her two hundred pound suit wasn't *criss* anyway. It just didn't have the sexy fit of the one Dee was wearing. And that meant all the guys at the upcoming wedding would be eyeing her cousin and not her.

'You get that down Soho Road?' Jazz asked, to see if her guess had been right.

Dee looked down at her outfit.

'Yeah – wicked innit?' she declared in her Brummie twang.

'*Yeah – wicked innit,*' mimicked Jazz, laughing.

'Don't be dissin' my accent . . . Us Handsworth girls are ruff, man . . .'

'Only jokin' with you,' laughed Jazz. 'I'm just jealous – all the guys are gonna be checkin' *you* out when we hit the dancefloor . . .'

'They gonna be checkin' for both of us, Jazz. *Believe* . . .'

'If they ain't got too drunk on Bacardi . . .'

Dee got off her cousin's bed and stood in front of the mirror admiring herself. Her coloured contact lenses complimented the suit and the highlights in her hair were the bomb. She turned to Jazz.

'I wish we could get drunk. Man, I hate weddings . . .'

'I like the *weddings* themselves,' replied Jazz. 'It's the

piss-up that I hate. All the *man* get to do what they like and we have to drink warm juice and that . . .'

'*It is not the respecting, innit, for the girl to be drinkin . . .*' said Dee, imitating her dad.

Both cousins laughed. Jazz stood too and straightened her outfit.

'Come on, let's see if we can sneak out. I wanna fag.'

'Ain't you given up yet?' asked Dee.

'Nah – *you*?'

'Nope.'

Downstairs, it was the night before Jazz's brother's wedding to a girl from Birmingham called Jagwant. Danny was Jazz's oldest brother, twenty-three and had just finished a degree in Business Studies. She had two more brothers, Steven, who was twenty-one and Karam, nineteen; and a younger sister, Manpreet, who was thirteen, two years younger than Jazz. Dee and Jazz were standing in the garden, in front of a giant marquee that had been erected the day before and was now full of the men in the family, all drinking beer and picking at plates of food that sat on rows of trestle tables. It was a humid Saturday evening and insects buzzed around the revellers as they listened to the bhangra coming out of a specially hired system, complete with DJ.

'Man, even the tunes are about guys,' complained Dee, as the DJ dropped his next selection.

The early evening air vibrated to the siren effect that the DJ employed before the familiar refrain echoed out of the giant speaker boxes.

'*Putth Jattah Deh . . . Putth Jattah Deh . . .*'

Jazz grabbed her cousin by the arm and pulled her into the driveway, past the open door of the garage where the women had set up two gas powered stoves, busy cooking and heating up food for everyone. Avoiding her mum, and a conversation with her senile great aunt, Pritam Kaur, Jazz led Dee out into the street.

'Let's go for a walk round the corner,' she suggested. 'That way no one can see us . . .'

'Where's Danny then?' asked Dee, as they made their way down the road, past a row of six detached houses, and round to the left, into a quiet tree-lined avenue.

'He's in there somewhere, trying to avoid getting pissed, I reckon.'

'Won't do no good if he's got a hangover tomorrow, man. At the *milni* and then the ceremony . . .'

The *milni* was where the two families met and exchanged blessings before the *anand karaj*, or marriage ceremony. Jazz knew that if her brother got too drunk he'd be a mess the next day.

'He'll be fine. My dad won't let him get too pissed.'

'Can you imagine that, Jazz. A hungover bridegroom at the temple – man, the in-laws would have field day, innit?'

Jazz agreed and then opened the tiny gold handbag that she was carrying. It was small but roomy enough, just, to hold a ten pack of Silk Cut, a lighter, her mobile and two miniature bottles of vodka, one of which she gave to her cousin.

'You sneaky little cow . . .' exclaimed Dee, opening the bottle and gulping the vodka down in one go.

'*Easy*, Cos . . . You'll get a reputation . . .'

'Like I ain't got one already . . .' laughed Dee.

'Yeah but that's with your friends on Soho Road, Dee. Not in the family,' Jazz reminded her.

'*Deff' that* . . . If my dad seen me now he'd throw me out of the house, man.'

'Well then let's make sure no one sees us. What they can't see . .'

The cousins lit up a cigarette each and smoked, keeping an eye out for anyone that might be driving by. Jazz was confident no one would see them though. The avenue was at the back of the house and the main road was to the front. Anyone arriving for the wedding would drive up along the main road. It was the route Jazz always took to have a crafty fag. They walked to the end of the tree-lined avenue before turning left, walking into a small playground which stood next to a public swimming baths. Ahead of them, on the road, a car sat parked, its doors open and loud reggae music blasting from its speakers. Jazz smiled.

'It's Jamie and Reese,' she told her cousin.

'*Who?*'

'Lads from school,' explained Jazz.

'So how come they got a *car* then?' asked Dee.

'Jamie's brother must be driving. *David* – he's Karam's mate.'

'*White* boys . . . ?'

'Yeah, and black – what's wrong with that?'

Dee shrugged.

'Nuttin', I s'pose . . .' she replied.

'Come on – let's see what they're up to.'

Jazz led the way to the car, and Dee watched as a big black guy got out of the car and gave her cousin a bear hug.

'Sister, sister – you look *hot*!' he said.

'Reese – this is my cousin, Dee. From Brum.'

Jazz nodded at Dee who smiled shyly.

'Dee – this is Reese. From school.'

Dee saw two white lads get out of the car. One of them was well cute.

'And this,' continued Jazz, 'is David and Jamie.'

'Hi,' said Dee. Jamie, the cute one, smiled and Dee relaxed a bit. She didn't know *any* white boys at all and she felt a bit curious.

'Thought *you'd* be tied to the kitchen sink and that . . .' said David, laughing at his own joke.

'Needed to get out for a fag,' replied Jazz.

'Where's Karam – down the pub?' asked David of his friend.

'Not yet – they's headin' that way in a bit though – down the Horse, I think.'

'Cool – I might go see him down there,' replied David.

'Wanna smoke?' asked Reese, reaching for his Rizla.

'Got to go home,' Jazz told him.

Reese smiled broadly as he pulled sheets of paper from the packet. 'Why?'

'*Wedding*, you divv. We got shit to do, man . . .'

'Sack that – can't you get out for a couple of hours . . . ?'

Jazz shot Dee a quick glance before asking Reese what they'd need a couple of hours for.

'Come down the club, man. My uncle's on the door. It's bhangra – you'll love it . . .' replied Reese.

'Shit man – it's Rishi Rich live P.A, innit?' said Jazz, remembering a flyer that she'd been handed at school.

'I dunno, man,' grinned Reese. 'All that shit sound the same to me, y'know . . .'

'Fuck off, you knob – bhangra's the best!' Jazz laughed.

Dee looked at her cousin and smiled. A bhangra gig sounded like fun but if they got caught they were going to get murdered. As if to emphasise the point, Buju Banton's *Murderer* kicked out of the bass bins of David's car.

'This tune's *old*, man,' said Dee. Mainly to Jamie.

'Oldest and *baddest*,' laughed Jamie. 'So what do you get up to then?'

Dee grinned.

'Oh, y'know – this and that . . .'

'So come down to the gig. Let us show you how to party . . .'

'Ain't *nuttin'* you could teach Dee 'bout *partyin'*,' said Jazz.

'So what you sayin', then?' asked Reese.

Jazz looked at her cousin and then back at Reese.

'Let us pop home first – see if we can get out without being seen. Make up an excuse and that,' she replied.

'We're gonna chill here for a bit anyway,' Reese told her. 'Give you half an hour – call me either way, sister.'

'Cool,' said Jazz, grabbing Dee's arm and heading home.

The car was full of smoke as it cruised slowly into the city centre. Jazz and Dee were in the back with Jamie, with David driving and Reese building big spliffs in the passenger seat. Jazz had told her mum that she and Dee were going to get an early night, ready for the big day. Her mum had just shrugged, too busy with guests and cooking to worry about what her daughter was up to.

To seal the blag, Jazz had moaned about little kids running in and out of her bedroom and told her mum that she was going to lock the door so that she and Dee could get some proper sleep. Her mum had waved her hands at that too and scuttled off to sort out more food for the men. Jazz then locked her door from the outside and led Dee out of the house. Not that anyone noticed. Everyone was far too busy. Result . . .

The club sat on the edge of the city centre and as they

pulled into its crowded car park, Jazz noticed that everyone waiting in the queue seemed to be Asian. David parked the car so that it was blocking off three others and they all got out.

'You can't leave it there,' said Jazz. 'What if them man want to leave?'

'They can wait,' grinned David, lighting up a cigarette.

The group walked over to the door where Reese hugged his uncle.

'Easy Uncle Teddy!'

'Yes, Reese! What you doin' here?' replied the doorman.

'Just comin' in for a quick drink . . .' Reese said, gesturing at the rest of them with his arm.

'Your mum know you're out?'

Reese kissed his teeth and asked if they could go inside. His uncle smiled. 'How old are the girls?' he asked.

'Old enough, man!' protested Reese.

His uncle shook his head and gestured them in with a wave of his arm. 'Just don't cause no fuss, man,' he said.

'Never!' replied Reese, pretending to be hurt at the suggestion.

As the people waiting to pay made comments and swore, Reese led Jazz, Dee and the two brothers into the club, nodding at the other bouncers, and hugging two more of his uncles, Dave and Tyrell.

'Are *all* your uncles doormen?' asked Jazz.

'Yeah – one of my aunts too. Oh *and* my dad . . .'

The door that led from the reception area into the main room opened and a blast of warm, humid air hit Jazz in the face. The place was heaving. They walked in slowly, trying to get across the packed dancefloor to the bar as loud bhangra music made their ears pop. Up in the DJ booth, next to the DJ, was an MC, holding a mic close to his mouth and urging the crowd to enjoy themselves. Arms, feet and bums got in the way, as they bulldozed themselves closer to the bar, finding a spot that was relatively empty just to the side. The girls stood against a wall as David and Jamie went to the bar with their orders. Reese stood and chatted to yet another uncle and a cousin as the MC introduced the next DJ, a reggae specialist, and a piercing siren echoed through the air .. A Sean Paul tune began to filter through the sound system as the girls stood and grinned at each other.

'Wicked!' said Dee, watching the dancers react to the change in music, some of them dancing on and others shaking their heads. Next to the girls, a gang of four Asian lads was staring at them. One of the lads went to the bar but the other three started to cuss.

'Thought dis was a *bhangra* do, man . . .' said the shortest one. He was wearing tapered black trousers and a white shirt, with a gold chain hanging outside his collar. His head was shaved, save for two lines of hair running from his temples around to the back of his head.

One of his friends, taller, with shoulder length, curly hair, grinned sarcastically before replying.

'Fuckin' black man music, innit. To keep the *kaleh* happy . . .'

'Sack that, Surj,' said the shorter lad. 'This is an *Asian* do . . .'

'Yeah,' added another of the gang, this one wearing a beanie and sporting a thin goatee beard. 'We never came for no *nigger* music . . .'

The taller one, Surj, told his mates to chill as Jazz gave Dee a disapproving look.

'Check them,' she shouted above the music. 'They talk like they is black but then they *diss* black people . . . hypocrites.'

Dee shrugged. 'It is supposed to be a bhangra gig though, innit,' she replied.

'*So*? Don't mean they can't play no reggae or R'n'B, does it?' said Jazz.

Dee shrugged again and started to move slowly to the rhythm as David and Jamie came back with their drinks. Jazz glanced at the Asian lads as Jamie handed Dee her brandy and Coke. The taller one, Surj, scowled and whispered something to the one in the hat, who looked over and shook his head in disgust. Jazz froze for a minute. She'd seen Asian lads take exception to Asian girls out with white lads, and black lads before. Just as she was thinking it, Reese turned round and put his hand on her shoulder, leaning in to talk. Jazz looked at the Asian lads again. The tallest one was seething now, his face set in a scowl. She didn't hear what Reese was saying, she was nodding just to be polite. The Asian lads looked over again before moving off to stand in another part of the club. As she watched them go, Jazz relaxed a bit, taking a big swig of her drink.

An hour later, Dee was pissed and dancing with Jamie to R'n'B, as Jazz and Reese stood gossiping about school and friends. The MC introduced the live P.A. and the DJ began to spin a bhangra tune. All of a sudden the dancefloor was flooded with Asian lads, including the lads who had given Reese and Jamie dirty looks by the bar. Jazz watched as the same lads now jostled past Jamie, shouldering him out of the way and challenging him to respond with cold stares. Reese noticed too and stepped towards his friend as Surj, the taller lad, began to shout at Dee. Jazz moved closer as the crowd parted and stood to watch the argument. She caught what Surj was saying mid-sentence.

'. . . respect for your people, man. You should be ashamed . . . !'

'Why don't you get lost!' replied Dee. 'Ain't none of your business anyways, you skinny rat . . .'

Some of the crowd laughed at Surj as his eyes blazed.

'Dancin' wid white bwoi! Fuckin' slag . . .'

'Knockin' round wid niggers too,' added Surj's friend.

Jazz saw Reese tense up and wade into the argument.

'Who you callin' *nigger*, bwoi?' he demanded.

The shorter Asian kid was holding a bottle of lager behind his back and as Reese stepped in he flipped it over so that the contents spilled to the floor.

'Fuck you want, you monkey?' he snarled.

From the doorway Jazz saw the bouncers coming towards them. The short Asian lad swore at Reese in Punjabi and then tried to hit him in the face with the beer bottle. Reese saw it coming and ducked underneath it, bringing his fist up into the face of the Asian lad, who hit the ground. Dee screamed as Surj head butted Jamie, splitting the skin across his nose.

Then all hell broke loose for about a minute. Reese jumped on Surj and the doormen grabbed them both, trying to separate them. Jamie was dragged outside by Dee and David, as more Asian lads joined in, swearing at Reese and the doormen. A load of them followed Jamie, Dee and David outside, as Jazz stayed rooted to the spot, caught in two minds. Should she follow her cousin outside or stay with Reese?

In the end she decided that Reese could look after himself and turned to hurry outside as the head doorman, Teddy, lifted Reese in a bear hug and took him to one side. The music, which had stopped during the brawl, started up again as the MC urged the crowd to chill out, in Punjabi.

Outside Dee and Jamie were surrounded by a gang of six Asian lads and a couple of girls. Two more of Reese's uncles were caught between them, telling the gang to cool off. Jazz ran over to them and one of the girls swore at her.

'What *you* want, you bitch!'

Jazz pushed her out of the way and stood next to Dee, as Teddy brought Reese outside too. The Asian lads surrounding them began to bait Jamie, calling him a 'honky' and other names. Then they started on Jazz and Dee. Jazz began to feel scared and her stomach turned over and over. They were about to get battered. And then from beyond the gang, Jazz heard a familiar voice and her jitters stopped. It was her brother, Karam, with his girlfriend, Holly.

'You all best leave my sister alone . . . !' he shouted, stepping up to the gang.

Two of the lads moved away but the other four squared up to Karam.

'Your sister's been in deh, man – hugging up monkeys and that!' spat one of them.

'What's that gotta do wit' you?' replied Karam, grabbing the lad by his throat and throwing him to the ground.

The other lads began to scuffle, throwing wild punches at anything and everyone. Jazz grabbed Dee and pulled her away, as the doormen lost patience and waded in. The girls went and stood by David's car, waiting for the fighting to end so that they could go home. Eventually Karam, Holly, Reese and Jamie joined them. Jamie's clothes were covered in blood and his face swollen.

'You okay?' asked Jazz.

Jamie said he was fine.

'What you two doin' here?' asked Karam.

'Just out for a drink – same as you,' replied Jazz, hoping that her brother wouldn't tell anyone about what had happened.

'Best get home then,' replied Karam. 'They touch you . . . ?'

Jazz gave him a funny look.

'Who?' she asked.

'Them *bhangra-muffins* in there?'

'Nah – Reese and Jamie looked out for us . . .'

Karam smiled and patted Reese on the back.

'You okay, bro?' he asked him.

'Yeah – but why dem man gwaan in dem ways? We wasn't doin' nuttin' . . .'

Karam shrugged as David walked over.

'Dunno – they're just stupid . . .'

'We'll see about that next time I catch up wit' dem,' snarled Reese.

'You got your car?' Jazz asked her brother.

'Yeah – you wanna lift home?' he replied.

'Be nice . . .' said Jazz, looking at Reese. 'See you next week?' she asked.

'Maybe,' replied Reese, rubbing his face where he had

been punched in the fight.

Dee gave Jamie a peck on the cheek.

'Might see you next time I come over,' she drawled in her Brummie accent.

'Hope so,' replied Jamie, smiling through the pain.

'As long as all the bhangra brothers don't see yer first,' added Reese, only half joking.

'You don't mind, do you?' Karam asked Holly.

'No – not at all. You can drop me off on the way,' replied Holly, smiling.

'Best get goin' then . . . got a wedding to get to,' grinned Karam.

Dee winked at Jamie and turned to follow the rest of them to Karam's car. As Jazz got in she turned to her brother.

'You won't tell anyone will you?'

Karam grinned. 'Not if you don't, Jazz,' he replied, looking at Holly.

My Best Friend's Dad

'Hey Charlie!' I shouted across the corridor at school.

Charlie, my best friend, looked up and smiled. The gang of lads he was talking to, Reese, Jamie and Dal, started grinning and telling him to go join his girlfriend. Charlie swore at them and walked over.

'Whaddup, Anisha?' he asked, letting his shoulder bag fall to the ground.

'Nuttin', really. Just another weekend of nothin' but boring shit.'

'You do that thing for science?' asked Charlie.

'Yeah – like I'm gonna spend my weekend looking at books,' I told him.

'Tek that as no, then,' he said, grinning.

'Er . . . *yeah*! *Anyways*, my dad was working all weekend and my mum was over at her sister's so I didn't have anyone to motivate my arse.'

I nodded to a couple of girls who walked by, Misha

and Tara, before picking up my own bag.

'Comin' to English?' I asked him.

'May as well – nuttin' else happenin'.'

We took a staircase up two flights to the English department, chatting about our weekends as we went. Charlie had been my best friend since we were like six, and we were real close. Not in no sexual way, though, although everyone at school thought that we had something going on. We weren't like that. Charlie was like a brother, I suppose. We talked to each other about everything, from who we wanted to go out with, through to how we were feeling and that. It was cool. Charlie's mixed race, or whatever you're supposed to say nowadays. Half white, half Asian. His mum, Sarah, is cool. I've met her loads of times. He doesn't see his dad that often, One weekend in a month if he's lucky. His dad doesn't live with them and he's always busy with work, although I don't know what he does, and I've never met him.

Thing is though Charlie has *never* met my parents. They ain't into me having boys round at home. I mean, they aren't really strict or nothing – not like some of the other Asian kids' parents. I've got one friend, Yasmeena, who's Muslim, and she has to wear the *hijab* and that. She isn't even supposed to *talk* to boys, according to her dad. My old man isn't *that* bad – but he thinks that I should be concentrating on my books and not my looks – and I'm sure that he wants me to find a nice Hindu Punjabi boy when I'm older, from the same caste and that. That's just what he's like. Charlie's cool about it though. He isn't that bothered to tell the truth. After all, we spend all out time in school together and it ain't like we'd go out and play football together, is it?

One of Charlie's big things is his dad. You know how people have one thing that makes them sad or angry or upset? One thing in their life that messes them up, maybe? Well for Charlie that thing is his dad. It's not like he hates him or anything. He just gets angry with him sometimes, like when he promises to turn up on some weekend, and then cancels at the last minute. Or the way that he only visits him on Boxing Day and never on Christmas Day. I mean, Charlie gets angry at his mum too, but never for long. His dad though . . . sometimes Charlie gets depressed for weeks on end if his dad hasn't been to see him.

Anyway, because I'm like his closest friend, I spend loads of time talking to him about it all, or trying to cheer him up when his dad's let him down again. I don't mind, I like being able to help Charlie. Everyone I know says that I'm a good listener and if you can't help your friends when they need you then what kind of person does that make you anyway? Know what I mean? Charlie talks about his dad a lot – and I mean a lot. After one of their weekends together, he comes into school all happy and buzzing. Like the day I'm describing.

Our English teacher, Miss Johnson, told us to sit down, and started writing a load of stuff on the dry wipe board. Charlie leaned over and whispered that he'd seen his dad over the weekend, Saturday *and* Sunday. I whispered that I'd talk to him about it later but he shook his head and started scribbling something in his notebook. In front of us, a lad called Jason Smith put his hand in the air.

'*Miss*?' he said.

Miss Johnson finished writing and turned round.

'Yes, Jason?' she asked, as Charlie tore out his note and pushed it across the table towards me.

'You know how that board is *dry* wipe and that?' said Jason.

'Yes?' replied Miss Johnson, looking harassed.

'Well, that pen you is using is a *permanent* marker, Miss,' he finished.

'*SHIT*! shouted Miss Johnson, immediately putting her hand to her mouth and going red.

For a second there was silence and then the whole classroom erupted in laughter. Eventually even Miss Johnson started to laugh. I was wiping away tears in the end, as she told us that she was going to find the caretaker, and to read from the book that we were studying. Nobody did though. Everyone waited until she'd left the room and started chatting. As if we were gonna look at our books? I looked at Charlie's note.

'You went to the football?' I asked him.

He beamed at me.

'Yeah – City versus Villa – it was wicked!'

'But City lost again, din't they?' I replied, remembering the sad look on my brother Nurry's face on Saturday evening.

'Er . . . yeah . . . 2-1 . . . but at least I got to see them play,' said Charlie, his face clouding over a bit.

'That's cool, then,' I said, quickly, not wanting to upset his happy memory.

'Yeah – my dad took me – paid for the ticket and *everything*. We *even* went to the pub beforehand and he let me have lager . . .'

'*Really*?'

'*Yeah* – he reckons that drinking is okay if you don't overdo it . . .'

'*My* dad won't even let booze into the house,' I told him, smiling.

'Then we went the cinema and Pizza Hut – it was wicked!'

'What'd you go see?' I asked, trying to remember the last time *my* dad had taken me and Nurry to the pictures.

'That new thing with that funny bloke in – *Jim Carrey*.'

'Oh, yeah – I wanna go see that.' I said.

Charlie had the look in his eye by then, though. The look that said that he was off in his own little world, daydreaming about his old man and what they had done together. I didn't mind. I reckon Charlie gets really lonely and I know for a fact that he envies the rest of us when we talk about going home to our dads. So it's not surprising that when he does see his dad, well, he talks it up for ages. I know I would.

He is a bit messed up by it, though. It ain't like he needs *treatment* or nothing – but you can tell that it affects him at school and with his moods and stuff. And it's understandable too. I don't know what I'd do if my dad left suddenly. And I can't imagine what it must feel like for Charlie – never having had a permanent dad around. All the memories he's missed out on – the kind that most of us take for granted: *like* Christmas morning. No, considering the life he's had, I reckon he's done all right.

After the lesson we went and hung out by the tennis courts watching some of the lads play football. We were talking about this programme that had been on the night before, about teenagers and drugs, but not for long. Soon Charlie started on about his dad again.

'You know what?' I said during a brief pause in his talking, 'I feel like I know your dad and I've never even met him.' I smiled.

'You think I go on about him too much, don't you?' he replied, looking all hurt. He's got these big brown eyes, has Charlie, and this 'little boy lost' look, and I just wanted to give him a hug.

I shook my head. 'Not at all, Charlie – honest – I was just saying, that's all.'

'Really?'

'Yeah, really.'

'You know what, Anisha? You're wicked,' he told me, making me blush.

Some shouting went up on the courts and we turned to find Charlie's mates, Dal, Jamie and Reese, having an argument with two other lads, Mo and Yusuf, who thought they were real bad boys. Mo was pointing his finger at Reese, who grabbed it and twisted. Mo cried out and then they all started on each other as a couple of male teachers ran towards them. Charlie stood up and shrugged at me.

'Best go see what's goin' on,' he told me.

'Don't get involved,' I cautioned but he gave me a funny look, shrugged and told me that they were his crew. With that he walked over and got involved, grabbing Yusuf by the throat and shoving him to the ground. What was that I was saying about wanting to hug him?

At lunch time we were sitting finishing our dinners when Charlie told me that I should come round and see him more often.

'Yeah – that'd be really lovely,' I said, as my mate Priti nudged me and grinned.

'It ain't like that Priti,' said Charlie, 'we're friends, man.'

'Yeah – heard it *all* before – it'll be weddings and babies next,' replied Priti with a glint in her eye and a smile on her face.

'Oh – *grow up*!' I told her, picking a chip up off my plate and throwing it at her.

'*COW*!'

'*BITCH*!'

Charlie burst into laughter.

'Come on now . . . temper, temper. You'll be stripping down to your leotards and mud wrestling next . . .'

'Yeah, you'd *love* that,' laughed Priti.

Charlie gave her the once over and grinned like a dirty old man.

'Yeah – I would, too . . .' he said.

'Perv . . .' I joked.

'Dutty Bwoi,' laughed Priti.

Charlie moved up to allow Dal and Reese to sit down.

'Easy ladies,' grinned Reese.

'Toys back in your pram now?' I teased.

'Lef' it. That Mo's got some coming to him, man,' replied Reese.

Priti rolled her eyes at me. 'You're like big kids . . . can't you just chill out?' she said.

Dal shook his head.

'Man can't go on in them ways . . . He was calling Misha a slag earlier.'

'You and her still goin' out?' I asked.

'Yeah – and he ain't getting away with it, man . . .' replied Dal.

'You lot are stupid – you know how these things end up. Someone'll get hurt and then you'll all get thrown out of school,' warned Priti.

'This mofo ain't never at school anyway,' laughed Charlie, grabbing Reese in a headlock.

'Gerroff me, man!' said Reese, all muffled and that.

We sat and chatted for a while longer and then the others got up and left. Charlie asked me if I was going to come over.

'When?'

'Dunno – how bout later?'

'You trying it on, boy?' I asked, instantly wishing I hadn't. It was meant to be in jest.

Charlie went red and shook his head over and over.

'Nah . . . nah. Ain't nuttin' like that sister. I just thought we could hang out, that's all. I got a load of new CDs off my dad . . .'

'S'pose I could come round after school.' I said, relishing the prospect of raiding his CD collection. Mine was getting kind of stale.

'Ain't your mum picking you up today?'

'Nah, not today . . .' I said.

'So, tell her you're gonna come over to mine,' he said. 'Ain't no big thing . . .'

'Yeah, okay – as long as you don't mind that I'm gonna call you *Priti* when I speak to her.'

'Could think of worse girls to be named after . . .' he said, grinning.

'Eh! You fancy her, don't you?' I teased.

'Yeah . . . I might. No big deal . . .'

We grinned at each other before getting up to go outside.

I met up with Charlie at the school gates and we walked down to the bus stop together. He seemed to be in a really good mood and spent the entire time talking about his dad. In the end I had to change the subject. I mean, it's cool that he likes talking to me but there is a limit sometimes? We ended up discussing telly programmes and music and stuff and by the time the bus arrived, we were arguing about whether *The Simpsons* was better than *South Park* or not. Charlie was talking up Cartman and I was saying that there was no better character on TV than Homer Simpson. I was right of course, but he just wasn't having it. Typical *boy*.

We got off the bus and walked down Melbourne Street, heading into the maze of low-rise blocks where Charlie lived with his mum. Their flat was at the far end of the estate and we passed Dal and Misha on the way, arguing outside Dal's mum's block.

'Easy, Charlie,' said Dal, as we passed. Misha looked on with a face like thunder.

'You all right, Mish?' I asked, wanting to know what was up.

'No!' she replied, glaring at Dal, who looked sheepish. He forced a smile.

'We'd best go in,' he said to me and Charlie.

As we walked away, I heard Misha call Dal a wanker and then the door to the flats slammed shut. I looked at Charlie and grinned.

'What do you think that was about?' I asked.

Charlie shrugged. 'Could be anything with them two. They was arguing over a Cadbury Flake last week.'

'Some people, man,' I replied.

Charlie just shook his head as we walked down a subway, which led under a block of flats and out into a grassed area on the other side. There was a gang of lads gathered around some swings in the middle of the grass and they shouted a few things at us, mostly dirty stuff. Charlie just ignored it and told me to hurry up. I lived in a different part of the city and suddenly didn't feel too comfortable.

'Rest yourself, man – ain't that bad,' reassured Charlie, after he'd seen the look on my face.

'Bit rough, though,' I told him.

'You get used to it,' he said, looking away into the distance.

We arrived at Charlie's mum's block and he punched a code into the access panel on the wall next to the reinforced doors. There was a clicking sound and the door came open. I followed him in and up two flights of stairs.

There was a musty smell hanging in the air and someone had left a half-eaten kebab on one of the steps. Charlie shook his head and picked it up.

'Hungry?' I asked, as a joke.

'Fuckin' idiots . . .'

I didn't try another joke after that. Instead I followed him along a corridor and into his mum's flat. There was no one else home. I went into the living room and sat down on the deep sofa, putting my bag on the floor. Charlie disappeared into the kitchen to get rid of the kebab, returning with a smile on his face and a packet of Jaffa Cakes in his hands.

'Biscuit?'

'*Yes please!*' I said in a mock-excited tone.

'*I do spoil you*,' he replied, mocking me back.

'What time's your mum get in?' I asked, before scoffing a Jaffa Cake in one.

'*Eh!* Check out greedy guts. What's up – yer momma never feed yer?'

I swore at him through spongy cake, chocolate and orange bits.

'She should be in any time,' he said, answering my question.

I swallowed my mouthful before I spoke again. 'Well then, let's see these CDs . . .'

'They're in my room,' replied Charlie, grabbing the packet of biscuits and heading to his bedroom. I stood up and followed, leaving my bag where it was.

We spent about an hour listening to various bands and compilations, with Charlie promising to copy some of the tracks onto minidisc for my personal player *and* making me the best cup of tea that I'd ever tasted. After that I started to ask myself if I was mad because I didn't fancy him. As Priti was always saying – Charlie was lovely. Warm, funny, clever . . . not a *lot* wrong with him, really. I was wondering what it would be like to kiss him when I heard the front door go.

'That'll be Mum, weirdo girl,' said Charlie.

'Who you callin' a weirdo, freaky boy?' I replied, pretending to be hurt.

'Well, you should have seen the way you was lookin' at me,' he said.

'Like what?'

'You *know*!'

I grabbed another Jaffa Cake and stuffed it in my mouth, so that if I went bright red, Charlie wouldn't notice. Only as I tried to swallow the biscuit, Charlie's mum shouted up the stairs.

'CHARLIE! Your dad's come round . . .'

Charlie smiled like a little boy.

'Wonder what he's doing here,' he said. 'He don't normally come round in the week. At least you can meet him though . . .'

I said that it would be a pleasure to meet his dad as I tried to swallow the last of the Jaffa Cake, spitting bits everywhere.

And then a man popped his head around the door, just as I'd stopped looking like a stuffed piglet . . .

'DAD! What you doin' here . . . ?'

Only it wasn't *Charlie* that said it. It was me . . .

Shopliftin' . . .

When me and David were little our Uncle Steve used to spend most of his time round at our mum's house. He was always asleep on the sofa when we came down in the mornings and sometimes he'd walk us to school. He's my mum's brother, and after our dad left to go off with a barmaid from the local pub, he kind of moved in. Not that my mum was happy about it. Uncle Steve was a bit dodgy, an expert shoplifter and thief, and he always had a load of stolen gear that he was trying to shift. He's still the same now. I got my last three mobile phones off him and David bought his car from him too. We used to call him Del-Boy, after that character in *Only Fools and Horses* because he was always on the make, and eventually he got me and David to do some of his stealing for him. When my mum caught on, she kicked him out, and now we only ever see him on the street, or in town, pissed or stoned.

He used to love a band called The Beat, who were around in the early 1980s, before either me or David were born, and when we'd come home from school he'd play their stuff over and over until we knew all the words to every song that they ever recorded. There was one song in particular, called *The Limits We Set*, which had this bit in it about shoplifting, and me and David used to sing that bit all the time. When I first met Reese and Dal I was singing that song and they thought I was a weirdo. But that soon changed when I introduced them to Steve and he gave them a stolen Gameboy each, just because they were my friends. They thought that he was cool and so did I. He was exciting and fun and he made me laugh and I suppose I looked up to him, so much so that I ended up nicking stuff for him.

It started when I was nine and David was eleven. We were sitting around on a Saturday morning, getting bored, watching the telly, when he came downstairs from the bathroom.

'I'm goin' up town, lads,' he said with his big grin that he always wore. 'You wanna come?'

'Will you take us to McDonald's?' I asked, being cheeky and expecting him to tell me where to go, like my mum always did, but he just grinned wider and said that he would.

'Just got a bit of business to do,' he said. 'Collect some dough off a couple of knobs . . . and then I'll take yer.'

I looked at David.

'You wanna go?' I asked him.

'*Yeah . . .*' he replied, quickly, getting up out of his seat.

I followed him up to our room and we grabbed our jackets and ran back downstairs.

'I'm just going to get me money,' I said to Uncle Steve.

I had five pounds saved up in a jar and I made my way to the kitchen to get it.

'You don't need that Jamie,' he told me. 'I'm takin' yer – it's my treat . . .'

I turned and looked at him to see if he was joking or not but he looked serious. I grinned at him.

'Thanks Uncle Steve . . .' I replied, feeling all happy inside.

'Now, how's that song go,' Steve said to me and David, before he started to sing it.

'*. . . Shopliftin' me likkle bredda. Shopliftin' me likkle sista. Cos all you got to do is just go forward thru da door an' when dey come fe check yuh out you nah go back fe more . . . shopliftin' . . .*'

We sang it all the way through the estate and down past the ring road that leads into the city centre. We only

120

stopped when we reached the clock tower, which is in the middle of the main shopping area, and even then we just moved on to singing another song by The Beat, called *Hands Off, She's Mine*. By the time we had reached the pub, where Steve was meeting his mates, my throat was dry and I couldn't sing any more. He told us to sit on a bench and wait for him whilst he went inside and got his money. He took about five minutes and when he returned he was red in the face and looked angry.

'Come on!' he said sharply, walking off without waiting for us.

We shot up off the bench and ran after him, as he weaved his way in and out of the crowds and turned up an alleyway between two shops. 'Where we goin'?' I asked, but Steve didn't reply.

At the top of the alley we turned into a narrow lane where Steve stopped outside another pub. There was a tall man with dreadlocks standing outside and Steve started to talk to him. The dreadlocked man gestured over his shoulder into the pub and Steve walked in. Me and David stood around outside, feeling lost.

'What do you think he's doin'?' David asked me.

'I dunno . . . maybe he's lookin' for someone,' I replied.

'Who?'

'I *dunno* . . . you ask some stupid questions, man.'

'Get lost, you knob,' said David, balling his fists, like he does when he got angry.

I looked at him and then looked away. Not that I was scared of my brother – we were always fighting – but he was bigger than me and I didn't want to get beaten up again. Not in the middle of town. The bloke with the dreads smiled at us and asked us if we were waiting for Steve.

'Er . . . yeah,' I said, quietly, wondering who he was.

David asked him straight out.

'I'm a mate of his,' replied the bloke. 'Leroy.'

He stuck out his fist waiting for us to cuff him on it, the way that Reese had taught me, so I balled my fist too and touched his hand with mine.

'Respec' my yout' . . .' said Leroy, as David followed my lead.

Leroy looked at David closely and then grinned.

'You mus' be related to that bwoi in deh,' he said. 'You look like a mini-Steve . . .'

I looked at my brother and realised that the bloke was right. I'd never noticed it before but David looked a lot like Uncle Steve, with the same sandy coloured hair and expressions and everything.

'You *do* an' all,' I told him, laughing as I said it.

'*Don't*,' replied David, sharply.

'Yeah you do . . . I'm gonna call you mini-Steve!' I teased.

'I'd rather look like Uncle Steve than you. You look like a *rat . . .*'

I was about to swear at him when Steve walked out of the pub with a smile on his face.

'You catch that bwoi, Ginger?' Leroy asked my uncle.

'Yes, rudes. He shit it when he seen me walk in . . .'

Leroy shook his head. 'Shouldn't buy tings he ain't got the money for,' he said. He grinned.

'Talkin' of buyin' tings, Lee . . . I've got some of them new Nokia phones . . .' Steve began.

Leroy shook his head again. 'Like them *watches* you had – the ones that stopped working five minutes after you put the dough in yer pocket? No thanks.'

'Come on Lee – that weren't *my* fault. Them watches was a one-off . . .'

'Nah . . . I *still* don't want one.'

Steve looked at me and David and winked.

'Tell you what dread – I've got some business to deal with but then I'll bring a phone by for yer. Special *discount* for me bredren . . .'

Leroy rolled his eyes and smiled. 'You never give in do yer . . .' he said.

'Hundred quid to you. Charger and everything . . .' replied Steve.

'All right – you bring one by here and I'll see . . . But anyhow you're conning me, Ginge . . .'

'Would I do that to yer?' laughed Steve.

'You'd sell yer own *mam* for a bluey . . .' laughed Leroy.

Steve cuffed him and turned to us. 'Come on lads – let's get some Mickey D's . . .'

'What's a 'bluey'?' asked David as we set off for McDonald's.

Steve stopped and pulled a wad of notes from his pocket. He peeled off two five pound notes and gave us one each.

'That's a bluey, Davy . . . go on, keep 'em. I've got plenty . . .'

Neither of us needed a second thought. We pocketed our money and smiled all the way to Mickey D's.

After Steve had bought us our food we ate it as we headed into the main part of town, where all the shops are. On the way Steve bought himself a can of Special Brew and he drank it as we walked. We only stopped once we reached Top Man, where we sat down on another bench.

'I'm gonna go in there for a bit,' said Steve, nodding at the clothes shop.

'You want us to wait out here?' I asked.

'Nah . . . I need a favour lads. I want you to keep an eye on things for me when I'm in there . . .'

'Why?' asked David.

'Listen, lads,' replied Steve. 'Sometimes when you ain't got nothing else you have to be able to turn one pound into five . . .'

'Into a bluey,' I said with a smile.

Steve ruffled my hair and grinned. 'Exactly. And then you can turn a bluey into two blueys and then five and ten . . .'

'How?' asked David, looking worried.

'That's what I'm about to show yer but this is between us, right? I don't want yer mam havin' to worry about anything . . .'

'I don't get it?' I said, looking to my brother for support. He shrugged at me.

'Look – what with that dickhead of a father you've got and her job and that . . . well, things are tough for her . . .' continued our uncle.

'But—' began David, only Steve cut him off.

'Listen . . . she don't need the stress and what better

way can you *help* than by earning yer own dough?'

I shot David another look before I replied.

'We're gonna get *paid* for helpin' you?'

'Yeah . . . A fiver here, tenner there. That way yer mam won't have to worry so much, will she?'

That was what did it for me. See, my mum worked really hard and she was always knackered and tetchy, and she never went out and enjoyed herself. Her entire life was devoted to making sure that me and David didn't go without. To me, what Steve was saying made perfect sense. We *could* help our mum by earning our own money. That way we wouldn't hassle her about buying us trainers and computers and stuff like that. I didn't even think about what 'helping' Uncle Steve actually meant, or why he'd be willing to give us money. I didn't care about that and, after all, this was Steve, our uncle. I looked up to him so much it was like he was a favourite teacher, telling me something that was right, and obvious. I was only a kid – it was only later that I understood what we were doing.

'So you gonna give yer Uncle Steve a hand then?' he asked us as we sat on that bench.

'Okay . . .' I said.

'How much you gonna pay us?' asked David.

'Depends on how well I do,' replied Steve with a smile. 'The more I make – the bigger the cut for you two. That's how tings work . . .'

I looked again to my older brother for guidance. David thought hard for a few minutes and then he stood up.

'Okay then, Uncle Steve,' he said. 'What do you want us to *do* . . . ?'

And that was how it started.

We learned all the tricks of the trade. How to distract the attention of security guards so that they would be watching us and not Uncle Steve as he lifted clothes, removing the tags with ease, and put them in with clothes that he had bought. How to take the same clothes back to the shop days later and get a refund, even though we didn't have receipts for them, or sell the stolen gear to our friends and neighbours. How to take three items into the changing rooms but only show that we had two, by ditching one of the hangers, putting the stolen gear on underneath our own clothes. We even distracted a shop assistant who was tagging clothes once, so that Steve could nick the tagging clip and use it on future raids.

We learned how to sell stolen phones and Walkmans to people leaving the pubs in town on Saturday afternoons.

How to watch for open handbags in McDonald's, so that David could distract the owner, and I'd dip in for money, credit cards and anything else that we could get money for. We even got blatant about it and ran off with trainers that we'd just tried on. Only we did that at small shops where they didn't have cameras, or out of town, in Derby and Nottingham, where no one knew us. All kinds of stuff. All of which earned us money. By the time I was thirteen I had nearly eight hundred quid saved up and hadn't been caught once.

The most money I made in one go was when Steve got me to get rid of a load of fake notes, tenners mainly. I even shifted some of them in school, at lunch time, until there was a big uproar and the principal brought the police in. Not that I got caught – they couldn't prove who had passed the counterfeit notes over and I wasn't stupid enough to try it again after they'd found out. I shifted the notes anywhere I could. Like Uncle Steve told us, no one gave a kid a second look when they changed a tenner, buying a bar of chocolate. The shopkeepers were looking for adults. Dodgy-looking blokes. Not kids. That scam made me about two hundred quid, I got rid of so many fakes.

Then David and me moved on to stealing CDs from

HMV and Virgin and that was even easier. They all had these metal strips on them and all you had to do was rip them off and put the CDs away. I cut slits in my bomber jacket specially so that I could hide them. And if we were worried about the alarms going off because there was a hidden tag, we just waited until a big group of people left the shop at the same time, and got out that way, hidden amongst the shoppers, and made a run for it once we were outside. We never carried the stuff *on* us, either. Steve would be waiting for us, outside some pub, or in a car park, with a car, and we'd ditch the stuff, change our tops, maybe put a different hat on, and go back for more. CDs were easy money.

One day Steve took us into town in another car and when we'd parked up, he opened the boot and showed us a ton of fake clothing. There were Armani jeans, and Nike hoodies. D&G shirts and all kinds of sunglasses. We spent about three weeks shifting that stuff to people sitting in cafés and just walking round the shopping centres or the market. We sold loads at school too, especially the Nike hoodies. At one point there were like fifty kids at school wearing our gear. It was wicked. And the more that we got away with it, the more confident we got. In the end we started nicking stuff for ourselves, too. On the way to school in the mornings, I'd steal pens and rubbers, and pencils and stuff, and sell them in classes. Just pocket change really, but still *money* all the same.

And it never bothered me either. My mum didn't notice because she was too busy with work and shit, and every now and then me and David would ask her for money, just so that she didn't get suspicious, only we'd leave the money she gave us lying around in silly places. The number of times she thought she'd found a lost tenner was *well* funny. I even started adding the odd note to her purse now and then. And all the while, in my head, I was singing that tune by The Beat. And loving it. I had money and I was being a man, looking out for myself, and Uncle Steve was the person to thank.

But it had to go wrong and it did . . .

We got caught in the January sales at a retail park on the outskirts of the city. We got there at six in the morning, with David telling Mum that Steve was going to treat us to a few bargains in the sales. Mum didn't even raise her head in her bed. She just groaned at David when he told her. It was a freezing cold day and the place was packed. Every single car park space was taken and there was a half-mile queue to get in. It was shoplifting heaven. We worked our way in and out of the different stores, returning to Steve's car every hour or so to dump what we'd managed to get. It wasn't just clothes, either. The number of people who were walking around with their bags wide open and their wallets and purses on show was silly. In the first hour I was there I lifted three mobile phones, two purses, a set of gold cufflinks and a really boom pair of Police sunglasses. I gave them to Steve who was drinking Special Brew in his car and then went back for more, heading into Next whilst David took on Gap. Neither of us noticed that we were being followed until it was too late, and after our fourth hour of stealing, whilst we were sitting in Steve's car eating cheeseburgers for breakfast, the police and the security guards hit us.

Steve was taken off in a separate van to us and we ended up in the nick waiting for our mum to turn up so that the police could question us. But while we were waiting, one of the coppers came in and said that Uncle Steve had admitted to stealing the stuff himself, saying that we were just along for the ride and knew nothing about it. They must have seen the surprise in our faces because they told us that they didn't believe Steve. I think they thought that we would admit to helping him. Only we didn't. When the police had left the room we decided to keep quiet.

'S'what Steve would say to do . . .' whispered David.

'But he'll get into trouble . . .' I whispered back.

'He's an adult – he can take it . . . I ain't going to no unit,' replied David.

'So we say nuttin'?'

'Yeah. If you open your mouth I swear I'll—'

Only he didn't finish because my mum walked in, looking even angrier than she had when'd she found out about Dad and the barmaid.

'You stupid likkle bastards!' she shouted. 'I'm gonna kill that fucking brother of mine.'

'I'm sorry . . .' I said, like that would make it all right. Some chance.

We got a ride home in a police car and when we got to the estate, Dal and Reese came out to see us and there was a big crowd. My mum kept quiet until we got indoors and then she battered us. And I mean she gave us a *right* good thumping. But neither me nor David cried or argued or called the social or anything. Mum was right and we were wrong, and we *knew* it too.

She didn't talk to us for about a week afterwards. And then the following Saturday she sat us down and said that she was sorry and told us that we shouldn't steal. We told her that we wouldn't and that was the end of it, as far as she was concerned.

But we didn't stop. After we found out that Steve had got a year inside, we decided to nick stuff for ourselves. Not as much as when Steve was around but still the odd bit here and there. And we didn't get caught again until David got nicked a few weeks back in a stolen car. But that's a bit different and we're both older now, too. My mum just sighed when David got nicked and then she went and had a good cry.

Steve came round about a year ago and him and Mum had a mad fight in the lounge. She was calling him a 'lowlife' and a 'wanker' and he was arguing that he did it to get us to fend for ourselves. It went on for about an hour until I heard Mum stop shouting, and then Steve, knocking on my bedroom door.

'How you going, kid,' he said, when I let him in.

He looked really pale and drawn and I asked him if he was okay.

'Course I am – stupid question. I'm still as handsome as ever, me . . .'

We had a laugh for a bit and then Steve said he had to go. But just before he went he asked me to lend him some money. Said he was on his arse and that he'd got some girl pregnant and needed money for a pram and shit. It was all lies, because he never gave me the money back like he promised and I never saw him with no girlfriend and kid, but I would have given him money anyway. I wouldn't have had it without him, and he had done time when he could easily have grassed up me and David. So I 'borrowed' him three hundred quid, most of my stash and he smiled like a madman and offered me a line of charlie.

'I don't do that,' I told him, but he chopped out two lines anyway.

'Suit yerself,' he told me, snorting them and then ruffling my hair for me.

He got up to leave and then something made him stop. He turned and pulled a minidisc player from his jacket pocket, throwing it on the bed.

'There you go, my yout'. . . it's got all The Beat's songs on it . . .'

And with that he left, sniffing and walking broad shouldered.

I still listen to The Beat now. And I still love that song with the bit about shoplifting in it. And Steve is still about.

Like I said I get stuff off him now and then, but he's not the same and he owes money to loads of people. It won't be long before one of those people catches up with him, too, and then he's fucked. I wish he'd just go away somewhere, but he ain't never going to change. He's just Uncle Steve and he's a blagger. Always will be.

And every so often I sit at night, with my headphones on and I sing. '. . . *Shopliftin' mi likkle bredda . . . liftin' me likkle sista . . .*'

And I *know* I shouldn't but I smile when I remember what we used to get up to. Me, David and Uncle Steve.

Carnival Night

Dal looked up at Misha and asked her what time they were supposed to be meeting Reese and Tara.

'Tara said they'd be here by now,' replied Misha, twirling her vodka and cranberry around in its glass so that the ice cubes crackled.

Dal watched a couple of lads walk over to the bar and order drinks. He turned back to Misha.

'So, we going to the dance afterwards, too?' he asked.

'S'pose.'

'What's everyone else doin'?'

'Reese and Taz are out for the night – dunno 'bout Jamie and Charlie – they'll probably wanna go . . .'

'Cool,' replied Dal, as the bouncer walked by, on his way to chat up some girls over by the DJ booth.

'Can I have another drink?' asked Misha, her face breaking into a cheeky grin.

'*Wha*'?' replied Dal. Jokingly. 'You is like a *leech*

sister – bleed a brother dry . . .'

'Fuck off you *knob*,' said Misha, laughing.

'Go on then – same thing?'

Misha grinned even wider and her eyes shone with wicked thoughts. 'Yeah and then *maybe* I'll give you the same thing that you got last night,' she said.

'*What* – kebab and chips?' teased Dal.

'Just get my drink, slave bwoi or I'll have to get myself a new man . . .' Misha teased back.

Reese and Tara walked in ten minutes later, grabbing seats as Dal went back to the bar, his pockets heavy with the profits of a big weed deal. He ordered the drinks, paid for them and went back to join his friends.

Jamie and Charlie waited for David to park the car. They were standing outside a fried chicken shop and Charlie couldn't stop grinning.

'Remember the other week when we caught that dickhead, Mo?' he asked Jamie.

'Yeah,' replied Jamie, drawing deeply on his one sheet spliff, raw as they come. No tobacco.

'That boy never even seen us comin',' laughed Charlie.

'Just watch out for him,' Jamie said, offering Charlie the last pull on the spliff.

Charlie took it and pinched it to his mouth with his

thumb and forefinger, pulling back when he felt the smoke start to burn his lip. He inhaled deeply, held it and then sent a jet of ganja smoke out into the hot, damp night.

Carnival night.

He sent the roach sailing in an arc into the road and spat. 'Watch *what*? That bwoi ain't doing shit.'

'Just mind your back, Cee. That Mo ain't got no sense of what's right, you hear me? He'll sneak up behind a man and put him down . . .'

'Not me,' replied Charlie.

'Look at what he did to Dal . . .'

'Yeah, well we seen to that . . . it was *you* that cut up his face,' Charlie reminded him.

'Never mind that – that was cos *he* pulled a blade, you get me? I wouldn't have done it otherwise . . .'

'I don't care about him anyhow – it's Carnival night – let's go get wasted . . .'

'Fine with me, bro,' smiled Jamie through the haze in his head. He was already wasted.

As David walked up, Jamie pulled some money from his pocket and walked into the takeaway, hungry for some chicken wings. The place was rammed and it took him twenty minutes to get served and get back outside, his forehead beaded with sweat like a smack head looking for a fix. He held his ice cold can of Fanta to his head and tried to cool down.

'Coulda got *me* some,' said David.

'You seen me goin' in,' replied Jamie.

'I'll get you some,' offered Charlie. 'My old man sorted me out a load of dough . . .'

'I ain't gonna say no,' smirked David. 'I'll get you a beer later on.'

As Charlie headed into the heat of the shop, two girls came walking out, both of them in glittering bra tops and tight jeans.

'Easy sisters,' said Jamie. 'Where *you* goin' tonight?'

The taller of the two girls looked at her friend then back at Jamie.

'Creation,' she replied.

Jamie shook his head. '*Nah* – you wanna come with us . . . *reggae dance*. It's Carnival . . .'

'Yeah but we don't *like* reggae . . .' said the shorter girl.

Jamie eyed her cleavage for a second before replying.

'How can you not like reggae, sister? That's like saying you don't like *food* . . .'

The two girls giggled.

'*Serious* . . . you wanna check it out – big sound system and music to mek yuh feel *nice* . . .'

He grabbed the shorter girl round her waist and pulled her to him.

'*Gerroff*'!' shouted the girl, but not with any real anger.

'At least gimme your digits then . . . maybe we can meet up after,' pleaded Jamie.

The shorter girl pushed him away, looked at her friend and then grinned. She turned to Jamie, pulled her lipstick from her bag and opened it.

'Take your jeans off then,' she said with a sly grin.

'*What*?'

'Take your jeans off. You can have my number if I can write it on your thigh.'

David, who had just been watching his brother up until that point, started to laugh.

'You'll have to shave that bwoi's legs first,' he told the girls. 'My man looks like Chewbacca wit' his clothes off . . .'

'Who?' asked the taller girl.

'The hairy thing off *Star Wars*,' said David.

'Oh right . . .'

— Jamie looked around, looked at the girls, turned, undid his belt and let his trousers drop. The girl with the lipstick wrote her number down his right thigh and then pinched his arse.

'There you go,' she said, before taking her friend's arm to go.

'I didn't even get yer name, sister . . .' Jamie shouted after them.

The shorter girl looked back and grinned.

'Jenna,' she said, before turning and walking away.

Mo watched the streets pass by in a haze of lights and people and sounds and smells. The humidity was making him sweat and his throat was dry from the harsh smoke that he had just inhaled. Yusuf was driving his brother's car, an L-reg Honda Civic with big fat alloys and chrome exhaust, and they were going round in ever widening circles, passing Victoria Park time and again. The carnival was packing up and the last of the stragglers were heading out, some going home and the rest off into town. Mo watched as groups of youths moved in packs across a litter strewn London Road. He turned to Yusuf.

'Go straight on, man. I wanna check out town . . .'

'No worries, bro,' replied Yusuf, dropping his spliff end out of the window and taking a long pull on a can of lager.

'There's a dance on later,' came a voice from the back. It was Mandip.

'What – that Rasta ting that was on the park?' asked Mo.

'Yeah – down that club behind the old cinema.'

'There ain't no dress code or nuttin' – we can just breeze in man,' added Yusuf.

'Yeah . . . sounds good to me.'

'Bwoi check out that girl . . . *BUFF*!' Mandip suddenly shouted.

Mo looked out of his window, which was rolled right down, and called out to an Asian girl walking into town on her own.

'*SISTER . . . wha' yuh a seh*?' he shouted.

The girl turned and gave him the finger.

'You *fit*!' continued Mo as the car cruised by slowly.

Behind them the driver of a black Mercedes beeped his horn.

'Fuck you want . . . ?' growled Yusuf, pushing down on his brake pedal on purpose.

The driver of the Merc swerved into the opposite lane and accelerated past. As he did so one of his passengers eased down a blacked out window and threw a can of lager at the Civic.

'*PAKI WANKERS*!'

Yusuf swore and set off after their abusers.

'What you doin?' asked Mo.

'Goin after them man,' replied Yusuf.

'What for?'

'But they jus—'

'Fuck 'em,' said Mo. 'I ain't got time to be chasing no stupid white bwoi.'

Yusuf thought about complaining but he didn't. Instead he took his foot off the accelerator and the Merc disappeared off into the distance.

'Stop at the Subway,' came Raj's voice from the back.

'Wha' you think this *is* – taxi service?' joked Yusuf.

'*Just stop the car man* – I'm hungry,' repeated Raj.

Yusuf pulled over to the kerb, cutting in front of a bus packed with people going out for the night. The bus driver slammed on his brakes, the screech echoing into the night.

Dal could hear the bass line as they approached the club. The doors were vibrating and from inside the muffled sound of a siren introduced the next tune. Reese walked up to the doorman, a short dread with hair down to his knees.

'Easy Junior,' he said in greeting.

'Yes, Reese . . . come in, man,' replied the dread.

'Got my mates with me,' Reese told him, nodding at Dal, Misha and Tara.

'Respec' . . .' grinned Junior.

'How much?' asked Dal.

'Five pound each my yout' – value for money *guaranteed*.'

Dal nodded and pulled out twenty quid.

'Pay the bredren at the counter,' Junior told him. '*Irie* . . .'

After Dal had paid, Reese led them through two metal doors into the main part of the club. The lights were off and the sweet smell of marijuana wafted gently through the air. The music was off, owing to the selector using only one record deck, and the giant speaker stacks crackled and hissed. Another siren screamed out into the darkness.

'*Raas* that's loud!' said Dal.

'*Sound* system,' laughed Reese. 'It do *exactly* what it sez on the tin, innit?'

Tara and Misha walked over the bar area, once they could make it out, as the lads walked towards one of the speaker stacks. The crackling turned slowly into a drum roll and the intro to a roots tune. The selector had cut the bass and let the tune play without it. A light came on and picked him out of the gloom. He held a microphone to his mouth.

'*Greetings in the name of His Majesty . . . Emperor Haile Selassie I. JAH RASTAFARI*!'

The last word echoed around the room as the selector restarted the tune, this time letting the bass thunder in after the second bar. Reese smiled as he recognised the sweet vocals of Johnnie Clarke, a reggae legend.

'*WICKED*!' he shouted to Dal. 'My dad plays this tune all the time . . .'

'*JAH RAS-TA-FARI*!!!!!!!!!'

The selector lifted the needle from the groove, flipped the piece of vinyl and dropped the stylus back down in one fluid move, never looking at what he was doing. The tune started again, only this time it was the dub version. The horn riff nearly split Dal's eardrum.

'*BWOI*! I can't believe my man ain't gone deaf,' he said to Reese.

'Ear plugs,' laughed Reese, pulling his weed from its hiding place.

'Nah . . .'

'Gotta be,' insisted Reese.

Around them people stood and swayed to the music, old and young and all different colours. It was still early and the place was only half full but Dal knew that it would fill up later on. Not that they would be there. The dance was a place to chill and get drunk on the cheap, enjoy a few spliffs, before they went to an R'n'B night. For now, though, the way that the bass line made his rib cage shudder was fine. Dal closed his eyes and let the beat of the sound system take over the beating of his heart.

'*Watch Babylon a run. JAH fire it a burn . . .*'

Jamie stood and peered through the smoke, looking for Reese. The music was making his ears throb and his heart beat faster. He walked over towards the bar where there seemed to be a bit more light. The woman behind the bar smiled and he ordered three bottles of Red Stripe. Then away to his right he saw Dal and Misha standing in a corner having an argument. He smiled to himself and shook his head. Grabbing the beers off the bar he walked over, hoping that Charlie and David, who were in the car doing lines, would find them.

'Easy you two – arguing *again*?' he said over the music.

Dal nodded a hello and Jamie saw that his eyes were blazing with anger. Misha didn't even look at him. He smiled and left them to it, knowing that Reese and Tara were likely to be close by. He was right. Reese grabbed him round his shoulders and gave him a hug.

'*Gerroff*!' shouted Jamie, struggling to hold on to the beers.

'*YES* . . . !' continued Reese, as Tara danced at his side, her head bowed.

'How long you been here?' asked Jamie.

'Long enough.' laughed Reese. 'I reckon Tara is gonna turn Rasta.'

Tara heard Reese as the music broke for a moment and she gave him a playful shove.

'Knob . . .' she said, smiling.

'Where's the others?' asked Reese.

'Gettin' off their heads in the car,' replied Jamie. 'They'll be here in a minute.'

'Tell you what, then,' said Reese, over the top of another siren. 'Hol' dis spliff and let me have one of them beers.'

He handed Jamie the spliff and grabbed a bottle. The siren split from the left channel to the right and then echoed around the room as the bass to the next tune kicked in. Jamie felt his ribcage pulsate as the walls and ceiling shook with the vibrations.

'*All bredren and sistren come together in a One-ness. JAH RASTAFARI*!!!!!!!!!!!!!' echoed the selector's voice.

Jamie took a deep pull on his spliff and wondered what was keeping Charlie and his brother.

* * *

Mo looked at Yusuf and grinned.

'*Nuff* girls out tonight,' he said.

'Is a good job I'm looking fine then, *innit*?' replied
Yusuf.

'Yeah – *whatever* man. Is *me* the gal check for . . .'

Yusuf thought about making a joke over Mo's scar,
which ran across his face like a fat pink worm but he
decided against it. Instead he checked his hair in the rear
view mirror. He saw some lads that he knew approaching
the car. As they walked up he got out to greet them.

'Easy Darryl . . .'

Darryl held out a fist.

'Yes Yusuf – what a gwaan?'

'Nuttin' . . . just chillin'.'

Darryl laughed. 'Like always . . .' he said.

'Where you goin' later?' asked Yusuf.

'Heading to that reggae dance and then I might go to
some R'n'B ting . . .' replied Darryl.

Yusuf thought about the ten pounds that he had in his
pocket.

'How much is the reggae ting?' he asked.

'Dunno – me nah pay. My cousin is on the door.'

'Can you get us in?' asked Yusuf, nodded to the car.

'Who you with?'

'Mo, Mandip and Raj.'

Darryl peered into the car, a big smile on his face. He saw Raj and Mandip in the back and knocked on the glass. They saw that it was Darryl and got out of the car.

'*Yes, D!*'

'*Easy* . . . I didn't know you and Yusuf was mates,' said Darryl.

'School days,' Mandip told him.

'You goin to the dance?' asked Raj.

'*Yeah man* . . . go and check out the sounds of Jah lightning and *thunder* . . .' answered Darryl.

'You may as well come with us then,' said Mandip.

'Come then,' said Darryl. 'Time is getting tight . . .'

Yusuf looked into the car and asked Mo what he wanted to do.

'Whatever,' replied Mo, shrugging.

'Might catch a squeeze on the door,' added Yusuf.

Mo grinned. 'In that case let's go . . .' he said, finishing the can of lager in his hands and throwing it out of his window.

Charlie looked at David and shook his head.

'I'm off my tits,' he said, sniffing.

'Same here, man,' agreed David. 'This stuff is well strong.'

'Where'd you get it?'

'From me uncle – he sells a bit now and then and he owed me some money,' David told him.

'Come on, let's go in,' said Charlie, nodding towards the club entrance.

'In a minute,' replied David.

Charlie got out of the car and watched a police patrol drive by slowly. He tensed up, sniffed and his hands went to his back pocket where his drugs were stashed. Realising what he'd done he brought them to his front. He looked into the car and saw that one of the coppers was Marcus, Tara's mum's boyfriend. He looked away. The patrol car went to the end of the street and turned right. Charlie didn't relax until it had gone from sight.

He heard the doorman greet someone and turned to see a group of youths walking into the dance, followed by a group of five girls. He knocked on the window of David's car. David got out.

'What up?' he asked.

'Come on – let's get inside,' said Charlie as the walls of the place began to shake and vibrate.

'Fuck me that's loud,' said someone at the door.

'Baddest sound system ina de *whole* of Inglan',' boasted the dread on the door.

Charlie looked at David.

'What we doin' here anyway?' he asked.

'Cheap drinks and you can smoke weed – and besides it's carnival night – we gotta catch some reggae,' reminded David.

'As long as I don't end up deaf, bro,' said Charlie.

'Can't guarantee that,' said David as they made out a muffled siren from inside.

'Come on then,' ceded Charlie. 'Let's go get deaf . . .'

Mo saw Charlie walking towards the entrance and touched his scar.

'Pull the car over right now!' he spat at Yusuf.

'Wha'?'

'*PULL THE CAR OVER*!' shouted Mo.

'Relax, man. I was gonna park up anyway . . .'

Yusuf pulled to the kerb and stopped. Mo opened his door and stepped out of the car, reaching inside his jacket. Then he pulled his hand out. He looked back at Yusuf.

'Keep the engine running,' he said, as the others climbed out of the back.

'What's the hurry, bro?' asked Raj.

Mo gave him a dirty look and told him to mind his own business.

'Be like that then, you dickhead,' replied Raj, as Darryl and Mandip asked what was going on.

Mo ignored them and crossed the street, heading for the entrance.

Marcus watched the Honda turn into Midland Street and told his partner to follow it. Ten minutes earlier they had picked it up – being driven erratically, with cans of lager being thrown out of the window – and had followed it on and off, making sure that they didn't spook the driver. Meanwhile Marcus waited for control to get back to him on the registration. As he thought about it, the radio crackled and control came on the line. Marcus grabbed it and spoke to the woman at the other end for a moment. Then he turned to the driver.

'Let's pull 'em,' he said.

The driver nodded and turned on his lights, expecting a chase. But as the car turned the corner the suspect vehicle had pulled to a stop. Marcus watched the front passenger arguing with the driver and the other passengers. He saw the youth put his hand inside his jacket and then withdraw it quickly. Throwing something away, maybe. Then the youth walked quickly across the street, heading for the nightclub. Something was suspicious.

'You pull the driver,' said Marcus, 'I'll check out the passenger . . .'

The patrol car stopped behind the Honda and Marcus got out, turning on the radio attached to his uniform collar. His partner got out too, walking towards the suspect vehicle. Marcus looked at the three lads on the pavement. Should he deal with them or follow the other one? Something in his head told him to concentrate on the lad heading into the club. He left his partner to deal with the driver and set off after the passenger.

At the bar Jamie and Tara were standing chatting. Or at least trying to chat while the music pounded their ears relentlessly. Reese stood behind them trying to get the girl behind the bar to find some cold beers.

'They're warm!' shouted Reese, trying to be heard.

The girl shrugged and walked off. Reese turned to the others and began to say something when he saw the doors open and David walk in. He caught a glimpse of Charlie, standing talking to someone but then the doors slammed shut and he turned back to the bar, to order another drink for David.

Jamie asked David where Charlie was when he got to the bar.

'He was right behind me,' shouted David over the top of another heavy bass line.

'What – he get lost between the counter and the bar?'

'Dunno,' shrugged David. 'He'll be here in a minute.'

Jamie shrugged, and before turning back to continue teasing Tara about Reese, took another quick glance over at the doors. They opened and Jamie saw Charlie arguing with Mo. Mo reached inside his jacket as the doors slammed shut again. Jamie's stomach somersaulted and he ran for the door into the foyer area.

He pulled it open and saw Mo holding a blade, threatening Charlie.

'*OI!*' he shouted.

Mo turned to look and just as he did Jamie kicked out at the blade. It fell to the floor and Jamie dived to get it. Some girl screamed and the other people in the foyer started to shout. Jamie ignored them. He was too busy struggling with Mo. For a moment his brain short-circuited and he got a flashback from some shit film – two men rolling around the floor trying to get to the knife.

He almost smiled but the second scream brought him back and he realised that he was in trouble . . .

Marcus watched the ambulance speed away and shook his head. He looked over at Tara and her friends, standing around in shock. He walked over and put a hand on Tara's shoulder.

'*Just leave it*!' screamed Tara.

Marcus didn't remove his hand. Instead he pulled her closer and gave her a hug.

'I'm sorry,' he said, as she sobbed into his uniform.

'You let me at that wanker and I'll give you everything I got,' pleaded Reese, looking at the car that held Mo.

All around them murder squad detectives and PCs questioned stunned customers as the rest of the people stood silently waiting for their turn. The club was closed off with yellow crime scene tape. The sound system crew stood to one side, disbelieving. Shocked.

'That's where all this stuff came from in the first place,' replied Marcus.

'*What*?' asked Dal, holding onto Misha's hand as though letting go would kill him.

'All that stuff *before* – you think I don't know? We checked up . . . *you* got stabbed – no one got charged.

The lad in the car has been attacked, beaten *and* slashed and he didn't press charges either. You think I'm *stupid*?'

Dal shrugged.

'*I'm gonna kill him* . . .' whispered Reese.

'*Yeah*? Even if you *could* get to him, which ain't gonna happen cos he's going to jail for murder – what next?' asked Marcus.

'I don't give a *fuck*,' replied Reese.

'It's just one thing after another – like a *bloodclaat* chain reaction,' said Marcus, sadly.

'Like dominoes,' said Dal.

'I'm *sorry*?' asked Marcus.

Dal felt a tidal wave of anger and grief well up inside his chest as he thought about Jamie.

'*Dominoes*,' he repeated. 'We keep putting 'em up and knocking 'em back down again . . .'

Trainers

'Food ready, brother!'

Mo walked over to the counter and collected his bag of spicy chicken wings from the harassed looking bloke. He grabbed a handful of ketchup sachets and returned to his mates who were sitting at a Formica table, already eating. Mo took his chair and opened the bag, lifting out a red cardboard box that was already seeping grease. He opened it and then split the sachets with his teeth, layering his food with the ketchup. He wolfed down two wings and a handful of fries before speaking. The chilli sauce that came with the wings sat untouched.

'I seen these wicked trainers . . .' he said, still chewing.

'Where?' asked Yusuf, one of his mates.

'Footlocker . . . they's *bad*, man.'

Yusuf took a swig of Sprite, eyeing a couple of lads as they walked into the shop.

'You already got about ten pairs of them things,' added Mandip, another of Mo's mates.

Mo thought about this as he ate some more fries.

'How much are they?' asked Raj, the fourth person at the table.

'Hundred and twenty . . .'

'Yeah right – you ain't *got* a hundred and twenty . . .' replied Mandip.

'I got half of it . . .' said Mo, picking at a wing.

'That's 'cause you never put your hand in yer pocket,' grinned Raj.

'Tight like a duck's backside . . .' agreed Mandip.

Mo gave them both a dirty look, gesturing with the wing. 'Just cos I got money . . . no need fe get jealous . . .' he said.

'Serious, though – where'd you get it?' asked Yusuf.

'Likkle bit of *this*. Lotta *that*,' replied Mo, acting cagey.

'You just t'ief it from yer dad,' said Raj. 'Me know you . . .'

A drunk stumbled through the door as, ignoring Raj's last comment, Mo finished his food. The bum tried to look sober as he walked towards the counter but didn't manage it. He fell into Mo.

'Fucking move, man!' shouted Mo, shoving the drunk aside.

As his mates erupted with laughter, Mo stood up and grabbed the polystyrene cup of chilli sauce that came with his wings. He took the plastic lid off it and shoved the contents into the drunk's face. The man cried out as chilli burnt his eyes. Mo stood and watched him for a moment before returning to his seat. As he picked up his next wing the rest of the people in the shop ignored the drunk and carried on with their business.

'Fool!' spat Mo, before grinning.

The drunk grabbed a handful of serviettes from the counter and left, sobbing and talking to himself. Behind the counter, the owner shook his head and forced himself not to throw Mo out of the shop. He clenched and unclenched his fists, counted to ten and took a drink of water before serving the next customer.

The lads were walking through town when the subject of trainers came up again. Raj asked Mo where he was going to get the other sixty quid.

'Don't worry yuhself, man. Me have a strategy.'

'What you gonna do – sell yer ass?' laughed Mandip.

'Move with dat!' replied Mo in disgust. 'Me nuh *batty bwoi*!'

A couple, who walked past just as he spat out his

homophobic words gave him a dirty look. Raj noticed, too, and tried to hide his own embarrassment but the other two laughed along. Mo pulled a single cigarette from his pocket and lit it.

'*See*? Tight nuh raas,' observed Raj. 'I didn't even see you go for that fag – hands like lightning!'

'Gimme twos on that,' said Yusuf.

'T'rees,' added Mandip.

Mo took a few long drags before passing the cigarette on.

'I can get that money by tomorrow,' he bragged. 'Easy . . .'

'How?' asked Raj for the second time.

'I'll just have to do some runnins, innit?'

'Yeah but what?' asked Yusuf. 'You ain't got nuttin' to sell . . .'

'Just watch me, man,' replied Mo.

Raj passed on the three-time smoked cigarette before challenging his friend.

'OK, then,' he said. 'I bet you can't have dem trainers pon yer feet by tomorrow night.'

'Bet you I can,' said Mo, looking surprised.

'Ready for that dance thing down Saxby Street?' continued Raj, referring to a party for under-eighteens that was being held the next day.

'*Easy* . . .' bragged Mo.

Raj looked at Mandip and Yusuf, grinning.

'So what's the bet then?' he asked Mo.

'You tell me – is *you* think you're the bad man,' replied Mo.

'OK, if you *don't* get the trainers – and you have to *pay* for 'em, receipt and everything – then I get that sixty dollars you got already . . .'

Mo looked at the others, hoping that they'd think it was a stupid idea but they were grinning. It wasn't that he couldn't get the money – it was just that . . .

Raj interrupted his thoughts. '. . . and if you *do* get 'em then I'll give *you* sixty quid . . .' he continued.

'And kiss my *raas* for bein' wrong?' joked Mo.

Raj gave Mo a dirty look. 'Just say yes or no, man,' he told him.

Mo thought abut it for a moment. Raj had challenged him and if he backed out, he'd never live it down. But if he lost the challenge it would cost him all his money. And he'd lose face that way too. Still, he decided to take the bet. That would shut the little bastard up for good, he thought.

'You're *on*,' he replied.

'Witness that,' said Yusuf.

'A me too . . .' agreed Mandip.

Mo smirked at Raj. 'Best go get yer sixty dollars, *bwoi*.'

Raj just smiled. There was no way Mo was going to get a hundred and twenty quid by the next day. He probably didn't even have the sixty he claimed was his. No, Raj knew that his bet was safe. He turned to Mandip.

'Looking like the drinks are gonna be on *me* come tomorrow,' he said.

Mandip nodded. Mo watched him do it and shook his head.

'Just wait, man,' he told him. 'Dem trainers gonna be mine . . .'

Later on, Mo sat at home and thought hard about how he was going to raise the money for his new trainers. He had lied to Raj and the others about having sixty pounds. He had thirty, and half of that was money that he owed to his brother, Shammy. Not that he was bothered by that. Shammy could wait for it. It was whilst he was deciding not to pay his brother that he got his first idea. Shammy had a portable CD player stashed in their shared room. Only Shammy couldn't remember where he had put it and thought that it was lost. If Mo found it and sold it, not only would he raise cash, but his brother would never know. After all, he thought that the thing was gone already.

Mo went upstairs and started to search the room. He began by looking under his brother's bed where he found all sorts of things. There was a porno mag which he looked at for a bit, a few cassettes and CDs, muddy football boots and two broken and battered mobile phones. But no loot. In the cupboard he found nothing of any interest, save another magazine which he stashed in his own secret place under the floorboards, and a bag of weed with maybe half a spliff in it. He left that where it was, realising that his brother would know if it went missing. At the bottom of the cupboard was an old shoe box. Mo opened it and found a load of CDs and a manual for the CD player. He looked behind the box. Nothing.

There was nothing under the wardrobe either, in the three-inch gap between it and the floor. Mo stood up and thought for a moment. Then, grabbing a chair to stand on, he looked on top of the wardrobe. Nothing of any use. He jumped off the chair and went over to some shelves that were set into a recess next to the chimney-breast. They were overloaded with junk but on the middle one he noticed a headphone jack sticking out from behind a plastic carrier bag stuffed with socks. He pulled at it but it didn't come. It was attached to something. He pushed the bag aside and tugged at a wire. Something was back there. He tugged some more and moved another carrier, this one full of underwear, aside. Behind it, still gleaming like new was the CD player. He grabbed it and shoved it under his own duvet, shaking his head at his stupid brother. Had he even *bothered* to look for the thing?

Mo hit the street about an hour later, the loot hidden inside his bomber jacket. He headed for the area around the community centre where dealers were sitting in their cars and crack heads appeared from the side streets – looking all fucked up with wildness in their eyes. He walked into the centre and found who he was looking for, a local lad called Mick.

'You got use for a CD player, man?' asked Mo, blatantly, not even saying hello.

'Hush up, man!' said Mick. 'You want Tariq to hear yer?'

Tariq was the youth worker and he didn't let people sell stuff in the centre. There had even been a few occasions where Tariq and Gary, who worked with him, moved on the dealers from the car park. They didn't care who they upset. Mo realised that he'd have to get Mick outside.

'Come outside, Mick – I got something to show you, man.'

'Gimme a minute,' whispered Mick.

Mo went outside and when Mick joined him he pulled out the portable CD player.

'That *all*?' asked Mick.

'Fifty quid . . . it's worth *double* that,' urged Mo.

'You havin' a *laugh*, Mo? Everyone wants *minidisc* and *Ipods* – them CD go for change nowadays . . .'

'*Come on, man*!' replied Mo, getting angry. 'I *know* you can sell it on for more than fifty you t'ief!'

Mick shook his head. 'I'll give you twenty quid – that's all I got – and I'm the one doin' *you* the favour.'

'Forty, man . . .' tried Mo. Only he knew that he wouldn't get that from Mick. It wasn't Mick that needed the deal.

'Twenty or go find some other knob . . .' grinned Mick.

Mo kissed his teeth and handed Mick the player.

'Just gimme the money . . .' he snapped.

On the walk home Mo counted up the money in his head, over and over again. He had fifty quid. Fifty. He was gonna have to do some quick thinking. As he passed parked cars he scanned their interiors, looking for something that might make him some money. Nothing. Then, as he turned into the maze of terraced streets where he lived, he saw a middle-aged man talking to one of the working girls, his car idling at the kerb. The man must be stupid, thought Mo. Standing on the street, talking blatantly. He walked nearer but the man just ignored him, moving aside to let him pass. Mo looked into the car and spotted a briefcase. The driver's window was wound down.

He kneeled, pretending to tie his laces and then, quick as a flash, he shot up, dipped into the car and grabbed the case, running off at full speed. Bchind him the kerb crawler reacted slowly, giving chase. But the man was flabby and moved like he was running through water. Mo was outside his own house before the man even made it to the bottom of his street. He opened the door and ran straight upstairs with his loot, shutting himself in his room. His brother was still out and Mo set to work on opening the case which was locked. In the end he had to use a screwdriver to prise the lid away but when he did manage it he got a shock. Inside the case he found a load of weird porn. There were three magazines called *Chix With Dix*, a pair of women's panties and a half-eaten sandwich in a plastic container. But nothing he could sell. He heard the front door go downstairs, realised it was Shammy, and shoved the briefcase behind his bed. No way could his brother catch him looking at that shit. He cussed out loud and went downstairs to eat his dinner.

The next morning Mo got up early and skipped school, dismissing his brother's daily questions about whether he had seen his CD player or not. He left the house at the usual time but instead of going to school he headed into town, determined that he would make up his money and buy the trainers. There was no way he was going to let Raj get the better of him. His day started well. He made three trips to Dixons, stealing CD-Rs and blank minidiscs which he sold to a market stall holder for another twenty quid. He had seventy pounds now and as the morning moved quickly towards afternoon he decided that he would go and check Footlocker to make sure that his prize was still there.

The sales rep showed him the trainers, limited edition black and silver Air Max, and told him that they were last pair.

'You gettin' any more in?' asked Mo, even though he

knew that they wouldn't. He had asked the same question three times before.

'Last pair. When they're gone, they're gone,' replied the rep, repeating what it said on a poster in the shop window.

'Hundred and twenty notes?'

'What it says on the ticket,' said the man with a smile. 'If I was you – I'd leave a deposit, if you really want them.'

Mo realised that he would have to. It would be no good if he made the money only to find that the trainers had been sold. He asked the man how much he'd have to leave.

'Twenty quid, non-refundable and only until the same time tomorrow.'

'What if I can't get back until the day after?' asked Mo.

'They go back on general sale. I ain't even supposed to take deposits but I've seen you in here a few times, looking at them.'

'They're wicked,' said Mo.

'So, you leaving a deposit?'

Mo pulled twenty pounds from his pocket and handed it to the man, leaving his name and mobile number. He told the rep that he would be back in the afternoon.

'Just gotta borrow the dough off me mum,' lied Mo, as he left. The man just smiled at him.

When he got to the coffee shop Mo worked out that he still needed fifty pounds before the end of the day. He paid for a coffee from the small change in his pocket and sat down in a corner, next to a couple of female students with shopping bags. He lit a fag and wondered what to do next. In the end the answer came to him. He watched as one of the girls went to the toilet and the other searched her handbag for something. She pulled out her wallet, smiled when she saw Mo watching her, and walked off to the counter for more coffee. There was a queue and the girl had to wait in line. She was hidden by a pillar. Mo saw that she'd left her bag open and moved closer, draining his coffee as he did so. He put out his fag and looked around. No one was looking in his direction. He pulled the bag towards him and saw that there was a shiny silver mobile sitting on top of the rest of the contents. He reached in and took it, pocketing it. He stood just as the other girl returned from the toilets. As she sat down he grabbed his fags and made for the door, smiling to himself. Sometimes things were just too easy . . .

He made his way to a bar which was known for being a good place to sell stuff. He'd been in before and had never had grief for being underage. The place was empty save for a group of Asian lads by the bar and a white man sitting on his own, playing with his mobile phone. Mo ordered a Coke, the bar man not giving him a second glance, and pulled out his latest bit of loot. He saw the man look up immediately and tried not to grin. The phone was brand new, with a camera and everything. Mo scanned the phone book and looked at some of the saved text messages. It felt weird to look into someone else's life but Mo decided it was fun too.

'Nice phone, bro . . .' he heard from behind. It was the man.

'Yeah – just got it. You lookin'?' asked Mo.

The man took a stool next to Mo and sat down. 'Mine's been playin' up. I'm Wayne by the way . . .'

Mo nodded.

'I'm Mo . . .' he replied.

'So, you lookin' to sell that, bad bwoi?' asked Wayne.

'Yeah . . . Fifty quid . . .' said Mo.

'Is it open?'

Mo thought about lying but decided that Wayne wouldn't care that it was stolen. He didn't look that stupid.

'Dunno,' said Mo, 'I just got it.'

Wayne laughed and put his hand on Mo's shoulder. 'Yes, bro – a runnin's dat!'

'You want me to check it out – try my sim in it?' asked Mo.

'Let me have a look first . . .' replied Wayne.

Mo handed him the phone and Wayne flipped it open and closed, smiling.

'Camera, too . . . yeah, man, I'll gi' yer fifty notes for it. Only if it'll take me sim, mind.'

'Check it out,' replied Mo.

Wayne shook his head. 'Not here,' he said. 'I know the bar manager and he'll give me shit if we do a deal that blatant. Let me tek it in the toilets and I'll check it there . . .'

Mo looked at the end of the bar where the gents were. He saw that there was no exit nearby. Still he didn't want to let the phone out of his sight.

Wayne saw the distrust on his face. 'Come wi' me if yer want . . . I ain't gonna rip you off. I'm known for me honesty . . . just ask the bar staff in here.'

Mo thought about it and finally he agreed.

'You ain't goin' nowhere anyway . . .' he said.

'That's right,' replied Wayne. 'But I'll leave me fags an' lighter wi' yer just in case – security like . . .'

He pushed his fags towards Mo and headed for the toilets. Mo sat and lit one of his own cigarettes and waited.

It took Mo twenty minutes of waiting and silent cursing to realise that Wayne had ripped him off. He looked around the bar and then walked quickly into the toilets. There was a small window above the sinks and it was open out into the alley behind the bar. A tight squeeze but big enough to get through. For a blagger. Mo felt his anger rise and kicked out at a steel bin next to the dryers. He swore at himself and then punched the toilet cubicle. He turned and walked back into the bar. There was no sign of Wayne. He asked the bar man whether he came in regularly but the bloke just grinned and shook his head.

'He just scammed yer?' he asked.

Mo swore again, grabbed Wayne's fags and lighter and hit the street. At least he'd have the wanker's fags to smoke, he thought. Only when he opened the packet, it was empty and the lighter was out of fuel . . .

Mo wandered around for an hour trying to spot Wayne. He didn't know what he was going to say to him if he found him but he still spent valuable time looking. But the blagger had vanished, along with the phone, and it was gone two when Mo decided that he needed to concentrate on something else. His stomach was rumbling and his head felt light from lack of food but he didn't grab anything to eat. Instead he tried to think. Footlocker closed at half-past five. That gave him just under three hours to come up with the cash. He didn't want to fail now, not when he'd done so well during the morning and the evening before. He wondered if he had anything to sell. There was his own mobile but he needed that. There was the PS2 that his old man had got at Christmas, only that would be missed. Other than a load of CDs and shit, he didn't have anything to get rid of. He need another scam.

He spent the next two hours walking in and out of the shops in the Shires, trying to find something to steal. But it felt like there was a security guards' convention on. They were everywhere. He had been closest to a good haul at Debenhams where an assistant had left a gold watch sitting on the glass counter as she showed her customer something else. Mo had walked up close, pretending to be interested in the watches under the counter. He had waited patiently for the assistant and the customer to look away at the same time. And then just as he reached slowly for the watch, he'd heard a loud voice behind him and the static from a walkie-talkie. He'd turned to find a burly, red-faced guard standing right behind him, smiling. Mo had coughed and muttered that the watches were nice before making a sharp exit.

He walked out of the shopping centre and stood by McDonald's, watching the afternoon turn into evening. It was quarter to five by that point and he needed to get the cash together. He walked round the corner, past the clock tower towards Footlocker. He had fifty notes on him, plus the twenty he'd put down as deposit. He watched through the window of the shop as the assistants stood around gossiping and the man he'd given his money to helped a young boy try on different trainers as his parents looked on. Mo turned away again and looked at his watch. 4.55pm.

There was an alley by the side of the store which led up into the market. The place would be closing up for the night and he thought about all the money that would be lying around as the stall holders packed their gear away into Transit vans. Maybe one of them wouldn't notice him, he thought. He walked through the aisles between stalls watching everything and everyone. Most of the market traders were already packed up, with one or two trying to get rid of their last few wares, mainly rotten fruit and veg. Mo recognised the tramp from the chicken takeaway buying a pair of browning bananas. He grinned to himself, tempted to ask him if he wanted chilli sauce with his fruit, but he had other things on his mind. He walked around towards the area where the clothing traders had their stalls, looking at his watch again. 5.05pm.

He noticed one of the traders carrying stock to his van and he knelt to do up his laces. There was no one minding the stall. Mo stood and looked around. No one was watching. He walked into the stall area and scanned quickly. There was a small wooden box sitting on a pile of sweatshirts. He picked it up and shook it. It had money in it. Mo could hear the change rattling. He tucked the box under his jacket and made a run for it. As he passed the tramp with his bananas he heard the stall holder swear at him in Punjabi. Mo ran on, down the alley and round onto Gallowtree Gate, past all the shops. He turned right at the clock tower and hit the side street by Gap, only coming to a stop when he was well hidden from the main road. He pulled out the box and opened it. Most of it was small change but Mo managed to get together twenty pounds in one and two pound coins. He put these in his pocket and tossed the rest into a green wheelie bin. He was less stressed now but he still needed another thirty notes. It was 5.18pm.

It was as he stood catching his breath that Mo saw her. She was coming out of a coffee shop, holding tightly to her handbag, and having trouble walking. He watched as she said goodbye to someone who was still inside the shop and turn to walk down past Gap to the bus stops at the bottom. Mo tried to make himself think about something else but all he saw in his brain was those trainers. He didn't want to do it but he had no choice. He looked at his watch. 5.20pm. He set off after the old woman.

She turned towards Footlocker and hobbled slowly towards the alleyway that led to the market place. Mo followed cautiously, keeping an eye out for any irate stall holders. He pulled a beanie out of his pocket and shoved it down on his head, trying to disguise himself. The old lady took forever to reach the alley but he followed her when she did and watched her walk up towards the other end. It was 5.24pm.

Mo walked behind her, trying not to make any noise. As she reached the other end, past a gate that led into the backyard of one of the shops, he jumped her, covering her mouth with his hand and dragging her sideways. The gate came open and he pulled her towards a stack of crates where he made her sit. He grabbed her bag from her and opened it, pulling out her purse. She just sat and watched him, wide eyes and silent tears. He looked away, ashamed of himself for a split second but then he saw the notes in her purse. Ten, twenty. Twenty-five. He looked at the coins. Twenty-seven. Twenty-nine. Twenty-nine fifty. Thirty . . .

He took the cash and threw the purse and handbag at the woman, leaving her sitting where she was as he ran for the shop. He didn't have time to worry about her calling for help. Footlocker was about to close. He ran in just as the man who'd taken his deposit reached the door to lock it. 'Got yer dough . . . !' shouted Mo, out of breath and blowing hard.

The man gave him a strange look. Mo took off his beanie and smiled.

'You still had tomorrow morning,' said the assistant.

'Yeah I know, but I needed 'em tonight . . .' replied Mo. He pulled out all of the money and laid it out on the counter as the assistant walked up.

'S'all deh – one hundred notes.' said Mo.

The man grinned. 'You have to raid yer piggy bank or what?' he asked jokingly.

'Just gimme the t'ings, man,' said Mo, in a hurry to get out of the shop. The old lady was bound to have gone for help and here he was standing just round the corner with his dick in his hands, waiting for a pair of trainers.

'It all counts at the end of the day,' smiled the assistant. 'What do *I* care where you got it?'

He ducked behind the counter and pulled out a box. '. . . Size sevens, all in there. I'll just get you the rec . . .'

Only when he turned, the young man and the trainers had vanished.

Mo walked into the fried chicken shop at just gone nine in the evening, careful not to drag his feet and mash up his *criss* new trainers. He ordered a fillet burger and fries. Behind him he heard familiar voices. He turned with his food to see Jamie and Charlie from school. He nodded at them, not wanting to chat. He didn't like Jamie. And Jamie didn't like him.

'Nice trainers,' Jamie said to him.

'Ain't bad,' replied Mo, walking to an empty table. Mofo was taking the piss, he thought to himself.

'You off to this dance?' asked Jamie, not letting up.

Mo nodded.

'Sweet,' replied Charlie.

Mo ate his food quickly, not wanting to hang around. He'd had a few run-ins with Jamie and he didn't want to get into another one without back up. He stood after a few minutes and made his way out of the shop. Behind him he heard Charlie say that someone was in a hurry, and then there was laughter.

Mo hurried on up the road, towards the train station. He couldn't help looking down at his feet every few moments as he walked. The trainers were rude, man. He wondered whether the lads were already at the dance, smiling as he thought about Raj handing over his money, the big-mouth. He didn't hear Jamie and Charlie approach him from behind until they spoke.

'Man's in some kinda hurry,' said Charlie.

Mo turned and stood his ground.

'Fuck *you* want?' he asked.

'Ain't so *bad* without yer boys . . .' said Jamie, grinning.

'I ain't got no beef wit' you,' said Mo.

'I heard you was callin' Tara a slag the other week,' continued Jamie.

'*So* . . . ?'

'Can't have that,' replied Charlie. 'Can't have no likkle rat-faced twat callin' my mates . . .'

'So *do* somethin' if you is so bad,' challenged Mo. They were all mouth, he thought to himself.

'Just warnin' you, that's all,' said Jamie. 'Don't bother bad mouth my mates again . . .'

Mo squared up to him. 'Or *what*, man?' he said aggressively.

Jamie looked at his friend and then back at Mo. Mo watched his eyes turn cold and before Jamie had time to react, he threw a right upper cut. Jamie dodged it and punched Mo in the stomach. Then Mo felt a punch in the side of the head, from Charlie. He doubled up and coughed. Another punch, piss-weak, caught his temple. He stayed down for a moment, realising that he had to do Jamie. Charlie was nothing. He waited a few moments and then reared up, using his head to try and butt Jamie under the chin. Only Jamie stepped back and caught Mo flush under the chin with a right, using all his momentum against him. Mo felt his legs wobble and then he started to lose it. The lights began to go off in his head, one by one . . .

The tramp watched from the shadows in the side street as the two lads dragged the third into an alley. He looked on as they left him there, taking his watch, his money and his mobile phone. The tramp waited until they were gone before he sidled up, his food in his hands. A can of lager in his coat pocket. He looked down at the third lad, out cold and bleeding from the nose. He recognised him.

And then he saw them. He knelt down and took them

off each foot. He looked at them in the darkness. They were brand new. He took off his battered old ones and tried the new ones on. They fitted perfectly. And then he saw that his socks were falling apart too. He looked at the lad on the ground. His socks looked fresh. He removed them, took off his own, and then put the fresh ones on. Then he put on the trainers.

He stood to leave then, but something in his head flickered. He opened his bag of cold chicken and pulled out the tub of chilli sauce. Looking down at the boy on the ground, he smiled his gap-toothed grin, opening the tub. He turned his wrist and watched as the thick sauce dripped satisfyingly on to the boy's face, running off the bridge of his nose and down his cheeks. The tramp looked around, saw that no one was watching, farted, and emptied the tub . . .

A note from the author

This is a collection that I've
wanted to write for a long time. Every
story, every character had been swimming around
in my head for more than a year.
From Dee and Jas in Bhangra Girls through to Johnny Too
Lie, the characters are based on people I knew or still know.
The collection is rough and ready too.
I made no attempt to dilute what I wanted to say in any of
the stories. I know that writers often claim that their writing
represents 'real life'. Well, I'm not making that claim.
I'm just telling it like it is - because I was there too.
Enjoy them and remember to let me know what
you think @ www.balirai.com.